This book is for you

You are currently not **being paid what** you are worth.

You want to know how to become an employer's **first choice**.

You want to take back **control** of your life.

You are dissatisfied with the **speed** of your career progression.

You are dissatisfied and want to take the **'luck factor'** out of your career.

You are dissatisfied with the lack of **opportunity in your industry.**

You want to land your **dream job – now!**

You need to **confidently package yourself** in the job market.

You want employers to **look for you** – rather than the other way round.

You want to know how to become a **real job magnet!**

Testimonials

"Adrian has the uncanny ability to get you to stop and think about the direction in which you're heading and what you've already accomplished in your career to date.

As a friend and a mentor I have had the opportunity to talk to Adrian on a regular basis over the years, and for those not fortunate to know Adrian this book provides the perfect platform to develop your skills and understand what it is you want to get out of a current role or a new one. Adrian provides great insights and very logical ways to map out your career in a manner that ensures you're looking for the right role rather than just any role."

David Parfect, *Head of UK Sales, Facebook*

"Adrian Evans has sourced very talented people for me in the past, and intuitively understands what it takes for people to get the job they really want.

This book is essential for anyone looking to accelerate and transform their career results, enhancing their confidence and understanding what it takes to win in a very tough market."

Frank Meehan, *Horizons Ventures, Former Board Member of Spotify and SIRI*

"Having recently looked for a new job, I found the hardest things to quantify were: what exactly do I want to do next and how do I get there? (Oh… and how much money can I get).

'Be a job magnet' is to be snapped up and either dipped into or clung onto depending on your current and future circumstances. Providing key insights into what today's employers are looking for, this is both an inspirational mentor and practical, step by step guide to improving your chances of success in whatever role or industry you choose."

Nicola Harris, 6-D Media.

"Thought provoking book - full of real life experiences that executives will recognize. Adrian sets the bar high for what's required to succeed going forward and advocates for a structured approach in areas that I would otherwise leave at the mercy of the 'luck factor'."

Reginald Warlop, Product Portfolio Head at Travelport

"Making your next career move can be a daunting step & ensuring you give yourself the best possible chance of success is essential in this incredibly competitive market place. This book will assist you to identify those hidden opportunities, develop your full potential & give you the clear direction you need to succeed."

Alys Mathew, Senior Online Marketing Manager, Betfair

"This book provides an invaluable insight into some of the less obvious ways for people to enhance their employability through exhibiting the behaviours for which today's employers are looking.

The adoption of some or all of the techniques and advice presented in this book will support career development and progression in an increasingly competitive and demanding job market."

Cath Possamai, *an expert in the management of complex large scale resourcing projects, talent assessment and selection, with over 13 years experience in multiple market sectors.*

"Life is too short to end up stuck in the wrong job. Whether you work to live or live to work, very few people end up in their dream job by chance. We all make decisions that shape our opportunities, but how do we know which are the right decisions?

I have worked with Adrian over the last decade to build a number of successful teams in different industry sectors and in this book he offers a practical guide to becoming both purposeful and connected in your career; helping you create the right opportunities and make the right decisions for you."

Graham Wylie, *Managing Director and Founder The Marketing Bridge*

"UK GDP has shrunk by 4% since 2008, for some that means sit tight and let your dreams of a move evaporate. For those who believe that the remaining 96% is a world of possibilities, this book is a great help in turning that passion into practical steps to get your dream job."

John Penberthy-Smith, former Chief Commercial Officer, Meteor Mobile Communications

"Whatever your level of coaching experience, or experience of being coached; you'll find 'Be a job magnet' a succinct, engaging and instructive book that will propel you on a fulfilling journey of self-discovery and career development. With the pace of a crime thriller, the readability of a saga and the simplicity of a master's cook book, this publication gives you the mind and skill 'sets' to place the power of change of your career and life proactively in your own hands."

Greg McManus, Founder, Sales Consulting & Coaching.

"Solid advice from a seasoned professional in an easy-to-digest format. Highly recommended."

Lisa Telford, General Manager with twenty years global experience in Technology, Media and Telecoms.

"There are millions of self-help books out there, mainly written by individuals sitting in Ivory towers who have theorised about the way of work and what you need to do to succeed. This book is different! Adrian's personal experiences mixed with an unparalleled desire to learn from successful people in sport and business is the differentiator.

'Be a job magnet' is an incredibly accessible book for individuals at any stage of their career, the advice applies regardless of economic environment and applies across a multitude of cultures.

Adrian gets straight to the point with impactful straightforward advice, the chapter on what employers look for, for me is a chapter everyone should read before an interview, as they plan their first 30, 60, 90 days and as they consider their annual objectives.

Increasingly employers are looking for the 'How?' as well as the 'What?' and Adrian's advice, guidance and tips for influencing, innovating and building confidence will deliver tangible success."

Wayne Searle, *Head of Organisational Development & Talent Acquisition at Cable & Wireless Worldwide.*

"I have known Adrian for many years. His positive approach, results and clear market insights enable him to share best practice to accelerate your career results in today's tough market. By reading this book you will be able to master the tools that will unlock your talents and help develop your full potential."

Mark Hodgson, *EMEA Director, Leading Global Consumer Brand.*

About the author

Adrian Evans is a headhunter, passionate speaker and results achieving coach. In conjunction with being an author, he is the founder of **'Be a job magnet'** - a coaching and career development academy committed to transforming professionals' confidence and results.

Using the methods outlined in this book, Adrian recently secured a candidate a 48% increase in salary package within the current challenging job market.

Adrian began his career as a recruiter and headhunter for a leading global recruitment company. Despite being in this business for over a decade he felt that he had not reached his full potential. He had reached a crossroads and knew that he had some important decisions to make. It was after the birth of his first child that he eventually found the confidence and courage to pursue his ideal career. That initial step was the beginning of an eventful journey that now allows him to enjoy each and every day of his business life.

Adrian coaches successful professionals who are committed to developing their careers. By enabling them to unlock their unique talents, they attract ideal career opportunities - thus reaching their potential. The end result is that they feel empowered, confident and inspired to enjoy the work that they do.

It was an inspirational teacher who helped a young Adrian to develop strategies to overcome the limits of mild dyslexia; he went on to achieve two degrees and believes that anyone can do and achieve anything they focus on. As an avid learner he believes that the best results come from targeted, focused and deliberate learning. Adrian has a deep passion for human potential and believes its actualisation is achieved through constant learning and implementation. He actively seeks out high achieving coaches in many fields to accelerate his own professional development.

His proven and practical formulas have been developed over the last 17 years through his successful track record as a headhunter and career coach, during which time he has recruited for some of the most successful companies on the globe and has advised individuals who have achieved director and VP level. He has a unique insight into the hiring decision making process and he has recruited and advised leading brands across many industries including premium consumer goods, technology, telecommunications, business services and the luxury brands market.

For further insights and proven methods that give you an unfair advantage in the current job market, visit www.beajobmagnet.co.uk

Caroline, Wishing
you Continued career
Success,

This book is dedicated to my children, Amelia and Matthew.
I hope this book shows you that what you wish for can come true.

Be bold enough to have big dreams, believe in yourself
and, with dedicated hard work, you can achieve anything.

Best Wishes

Adrian

Be a **job** magnet

7 secrets that guarantee you an
'unfair advantage' in the current job market

ADRIAN EVANS

Published by Filament Publishing Ltd
16, Croydon Road, Waddon,
Croydon, Surrey CR0 4PA

info@filamentpublishing.com

Telephone +44 (0) 20 8688 2598
Website www.filamentpublishing.com

© 2012 Adrian Evans

ISBN 978-1-908691-04-0

Printed by the Berforts Group, Stevenage and Hastings.

CONTENTS

Be a job magnet

7 secrets that guarantee you an
'unfair advantage' in the current job market

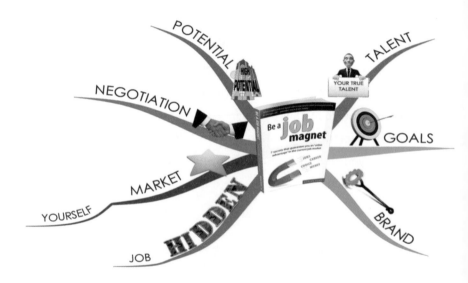

Acknowledgements

Writing a book is a long and involved process but one that is certainly worthwhile and requires collaboration with others. I would like to thank the following people who have helped to evolve a series of ideas and experiences into a practical and useable toolkit for those seeking further achievement in their careers.

Firstly my publisher Chris Day for his constant guidance and being a font of knowledge on all things book related.

Book designer Clare Clarke for her creativity and uncanny ability to translate a brief into a clear visual message.

Phil Chambers - the world champion mind mapper - thank you for speed of response and ability to produce such excellent mind maps that make the content so clear.

Thank you to Richard Wright for his support and professional insight and for taking the time to compose such an elegant foreword.

Simon Taylor for the case study and the key insights that today's employers seek when employing key talent.

Jeff Grout for his knowledge, inspiration and wisdom.

A particular thank you to Russell Adams, Howard Bell, James Nathan, Kath Roberts, Wayne Searle, Dave Seddon and Graham Wylie. Each one has tested the content, challenged my thinking on much of the subject matter and evolved the book into its current form. I thank you all for your honesty, ideas and guidance.

All significant projects require inspiration, strategy and continued motivation. Sue Stone and Gina Lazenby have been great teachers with a willingness to share a number of their methods that have helped them become bestselling authors - thank you.

To fellow authors Jo Owen, Roger Ellerton and Nick Owen - thank you for your advice during the early stages of the book development.

Thank you to Ross Wilson for being a key mentor, for acting as a source of inspiration and also for challenging my performance on a consistent basis.

Barry Lewis and Robert Spencer - thank you for your key career insights, planning tips and wisdom.

We all need shining lights in our world. I would like to acknowledge the following people, none of whom I have met, but who have had a profound impact on my thinking, possibilities and my journey of personal and professional development, Thomas Edison, Tim Berners-Lee - the inventor of the World Wide Web, Steve Jobs, who sadly died at the young age of 56, and Arielle Ford.

To my Mum - thank you for always believing I could achieve anything, your belief in me has been a true gift. To my Dad - thank you. Your values continue to impact my every day.

My wife Kate has been fundamental in the development of this book. Kate has been editor in chief and has dedicated many hours 'discussing' the content of this valuable guide. I would like to thank her for displaying patience, understanding and her constant support and for making me smile each day.

Foreword

This book is about how to take control of your career. It's true some people never will, equally it's true that for some it just comes naturally. However the vast majority, if properly guided, could create many more opportunities for themselves, make much better decisions, and in doing so build a much stronger 'personal brand'.

Planning, focus, networking, innovation, integrity, reciprocation, influence, confidence and action all need to be thought through and considered. The following chapters will provide a route map to do just that. This is an opportunity to develop 'a better version of you'; you may even have the odd light bulb moment!

It would have been all too easy for me to let others succeed around me or lose control over my career; I've seen many for whom that is true. Instead I decided to extract myself from a comfort zone and plan a future confident that there were longer term benefits behind some short term pain.

Richard Wright
Chief Executive, Archer Mathieson . Non Executive Director, Rees Draper Wright. Non Executive Director, Acre Resources.

After working at Michael Page, Richard spent 15 years building Martin Ward Anderson, a professional recruitment business, which grew to become a £45m turnover business with 225 employees. As CEO, Richard led the sale of the business to the Dutch staffing organisation, Randstad, in 2006. Since then, Richard has worked with other smaller recruitment businesses - either privately owned or with private equity investors.

Introduction - the aim of this book

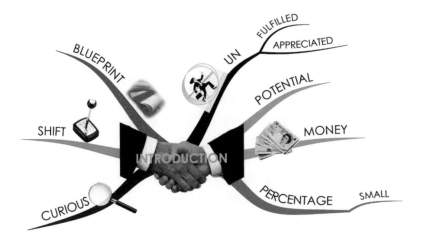

Are you currently in a job or following a career pathway where you feel unfulfilled, uninspired or unappreciated? Maybe you are simply just not enjoying what you do every day?

Your fulfilment at work has a direct impact on all aspects of your life from your self esteem to your well being, to how you connect with friends and family. I would like to share with you how I know you can enhance your career, so that it is shaped around the best version of you, and uses your skills, passions and potential to the full. Work is where you spend most of your daylight hours so why not aim to be happy and confident whilst developing your full potential.

There are some who wander through their careers without clear direction, just moving from opportunity to opportunity without a focus or plan. They may join the right company or gain access to a fulfilling role by chance, where they have permission to use their natural talents, but this is often short lived. In my experience, only a very small percentage of people get the roles that they deserve, in a company they desire and without having to leave a large percentage of their personality at the office door. Top achievers in every field strive to live their life and their career by playing to their strengths expressing their talents at every opportunity.

My purpose in this book is to provide you with the insights to allow you to unlock your talents and provide a comprehensive toolkit and framework of how to be a job magnet. This toolkit will allow you to make better career decisions, prioritise actions, gain recognition and build your confidence.

My proven and practical formulas have evolved over the last 17 years through my track record as a headhunter and career coach. During which time I have recruited for some of the most successful companies on the globe and given advice to individuals who have achieved director and executive level roles.

One of the key values I hold is candidate and client confidentiality. I do not intend to break that trust. Therefore names of candidates or clients throughout the book have been omitted or disguised.

To get the most out of this book I would urge you to set yourself a clear objective of what you want to achieve once you have read the book.

• Is it to clearly understand your career purpose?
• Is it to realise new career possibilities?
• Is it to understand how companies really judge high potential?
• Is it to achieve accelerated career results?
• Is it to discover your natural talent?
• Is it to develop a specific and targeted annual networking plan?

Acknowledge where you are currently and, by identifying a desired goal, you will have a new found clarity. Be open and curious to the new information presented and reflect on how it will give you an 'unfair advantage' in the current job market.

At the end of each chapter I have some specific actions points for you to discover. By undertaking these you will begin to create momentum within your career and this is how all achievers move towards their desired results. I urge you to take the time to go through each of these as I genuinely believe there will be positive mind shift changes throughout each one of the chapters for you. My chief desire is to leave you with a blueprint as to how to develop a more fulfilling, rewarding career and maximise your potential. This will allow you to take an 'unfair' competitive advantage into the marketplace and ultimately become a job magnet.

Enjoy the journey!

For further insights and proven methods that give you an unfair advantage in the current job market, visit www.beajobmagnet.co.uk

Q & A: What do successful candidates do that impresses employers...

Managing Director of Capita Resourcing **Simon Taylor** shares his key insights.

What common mistakes do candidates make when planning their careers?

Maybe not so much at the senior level, but many candidates in my opinion are too willing to move for what they would consider a decent increase in money, but in reality pales into insignificance versus what they could achieve if they stayed put. Candidates also underestimate how difficult it is to start again somewhere new and how much the banked 'goodwill' capital they have with their current employer is worth.

What common mistakes do candidates make on their CV and at interview time?

The usual boring but important things such as spelling and grammar unfortunately. Often they will also devote too much space to older and now mostly irrelevant jobs when more detail on the more recent positions would be more useful and make them more saleable. Presenting their jobs in a way that draws out what the tangible value of their contribution was to their team or the company in a clear 'feature and benefit' way makes it easier to map the value of a candidate to your own organisation.

What do you look for on a CV when compiling a shortlist?

Stability, good spelling and grammar, an element of progression within an organisation rather than every promotion coming with a change of company, and in a 'dead heat' something that sets them apart as interesting or a bit more creative than others.

How has a candidate impressed you recently?

By doing an incredible amount of research about my company and the sector both prior to and during the interview and selection process. This culminated with the candidate actually having a promise of business from a potential client despite not having a job with the organisation yet!

What key skills do you believe are essential for candidates to master over the next few years?

I think that people who can challenge the status quo, even if it is one that they created, will be increasingly valued. We are in uncharted waters at the moment and people who can keep critically re-evaluating the way that they operate and their teams operate will be able to demonstrate their ongoing value even through difficult times.

I also think that candidates need to take a bit more responsibility for their own development and career progression by engaging with their managers and employers in a 'peer to peer' way rather than either 'parent to child' or adversarial manner.

What candidates' behaviours positively and negatively influence your decision making process when hiring key talent?

Positive: Punctuality, flexibility during the interview process in terms of time and location, intelligent, perceptive questions, displaying some 'backbone', having an opinion and not being afraid for it to differ from the interviewer's own, really coming across as interested and keen on the position.

Negative: The inverse of the above, not having a compelling reason for leaving current or last employer, asking about the minutiae of potential package, any appearance of aloofness or coming over as ambivalent about the opportunity or company.

What advice do you have for someone wanting to accelerate their career development in the current market?

Put your hand up for more responsibility to take on projects once you have proven that you can perform in your 'day job'. Be prepared to take this on 'for free' whilst you prove your value before you broach the subject of financial reward. It is much easier to make a case in your own mind and to others if you can point to some demonstrable extra value that an individual has added over and above base expectations of their job role.

What depth of research should candidates conduct to differentiate themselves in the current market?

More than just being able to quote sections of my website at me! However, not so much that they think they have diagnosed all the problems of a company by speaking to a few people on Linkedin.

The best version of you

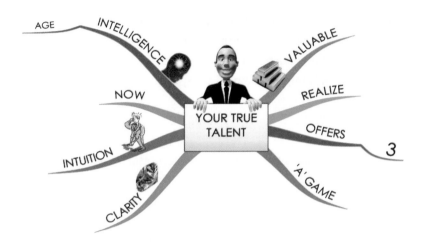

Secret 1

Discover the mystery to unlocking your true talent

You are a unique and valuable individual. If you take just one message from this book, it is this fact. Discover your unique talents and use your power to attract ideal career opportunities that will realise your potential.

1

Many of us are guilty of convincing ourselves that we cannot achieve our potential or that our career aspirations are unattainable. Very rarely do I meet individuals who are committed to the seemingly impossible goal of experiencing their ideal career.

Dare to view yourself as highly valuable

I believe in the current age people have forgotten how valuable they are and how valuable they can be. Despite one's individual success we can often end up feeling that our success was mainly down to the company's market position and the organisation in which we are part of and that it had little to do with one's own talents and strengths.

Well I have to disagree; every successful business is built and grown by people, not systems or technology. It is the people who have the creative ideas, engage with customers and make an organisation a living, breathing organism.

During the last recession most people I talked to believed they had few options and lacked career choice. There is a small group of people, however, who despite external events in the world, always believe they have choice and, most importantly, they use that choice. These candidates were still getting a minimum of three job offers and 20% + increases in salary. I will share with you in detail in Chapter 4 how a candidate achieved this and actually created a role that previously did not exist.

Imagine playing your 'A' game every day

What do Lord Sugar, J.K. Rowling, Richard Branson and Warren Buffet have in common?

1

Apart from being very wealthy - they love the jobs that they do and are playing to their strengths.

I believe that for a successful, enjoyable and rewarding career, you need to be playing the right game and playing in the right position; that is your 'A' game every day. You know when it's almost effortless to achieve something as opposed to doing activities that really are unenjoyable. If you can spend more time in the space you enjoy then the true you will shine through and you will succeed more and be paid more.

Have you ever wondered why it is that some people seem to get the right jobs and make the right career choices? It looks as if it just falls in their lap.

A friend of mine is a top ranking professional within the area of motor sport. At a very young age he decided that he was going to work in this industry and be a leading figure in his chosen field. This vision and clarity enabled him to focus his energies towards his identified goal. He identified which subjects to study at A level, which university to go to and who he had to network with.

I would love to have had such clarity at a young age. Personally on leaving university, I was delighted to secure any employment.

Can you gain such clarity wherever you are in your career? Yes, Yes and Yes.

The great news is that the tools are available to all of us to clarify our purpose and strengths. We can then reaffirm or adjust the direction our career is heading in, ensuring that we are fulfilled and rewarded in the place where we spend so much of our lives. It only takes a moment to decide if an action is taking you towards your goal or distracting you.

How to discover your strengths and key career drivers

1

Richard Branson and the other successful people I identified are individuals who spend practically all of their time doing what they do best. They have true clarity on their strengths and goals and utilise them effectively on a daily basis to propel themselves forward.

At an intuitive level discovering if you are playing to your career strengths is to ask yourself just how fulfilled and happy you are in your current role? To what extent are you using your unique talents? Take the time to identify your key attributes and career drivers.

Throughout my career I have often found it useful to utilise the following formula to identify if I am currently in the most appropriate role to develop my career. There was a particular time when I felt disillusioned and did not know why. So I asked myself the following:

1

- Was it the industry I was in?

- Was it the organisation I was in?

- Was it the team I was in?

- Was it my line manager?

- Was it the job?

- Was it the career prospects?

- Was it the salary and package?

I then scored each one of these out of 10. This was certainly not overly scientific but just my intuitive reaction. The conclusion I came to was that I was reporting to a line manager who I believed would not assist me in developing my career. We were mismatched in several areas, but fundamentally our value set was not aligned and this resulted in a large amount of conflict and stress. What it also confirmed was that I was in the right industry and the right organisation with the right culture.

This clarity gave me power; it provided me with choice. I was now able to decide what career changes to make and what could be left alone. I did not need to change industry or organisation.

Fortunately for me, within a few months, the line manager moved onto another business. I got his job and my career and life were enjoyable and rewarding again. Rather than just moving organisation or making a poor career decision I had achieved a very desirable outcome. I have utilised this formula with a number of candidates and they have been able to make controlled effective career decisions on whether to move from one organisation to another.

1

Your most valuable asset – your intuition

Moving forward, consider using your intuition to guide you in a powerful way to create more choice in your career.

Society and our education system have often encouraged us to only focus on the logical, and take a systematic approach when making decisions. However I believe we have earned the right from our experiences to listen to our intuition as well.

A compelling example of this is demonstrated by one of the world's most successful businessman - Warren Buffett. It is commonly believed that when he is considering the purchase of a business he asks himself three questions about the current owners that are based on his intuition. Does he trust this person? Does he respect them? Does he like them? If the answer to any of those questions is a no, then the deal is off.

When starting to craft your ideal career move ask yourself the following questions and document your thoughts:

What career pathway would you take if you knew you could not fail?

_____

_____

_____

What career aspirations do you secretly dream about?

_____

_____

_____

What career would you love to be doing every day?

_____

_____

_____

What would you like to have achieved by the end of your business career?

_____

_____

_____

This is a useful exercise to help make more effective decisions in both your career and personal life.

1

CASE STUDY
How to move industries...mindset, attitude and deliberate action

Moving to a new industry sector can be tough, many people do not even attempt to because they believe it is too difficult to achieve. A candidate who I was supporting in finding her ideal career move, wanted to do just this and change from the publishing industry to the telecoms industry.

This can be very difficult as many employers prefer candidates who have experience of the telecoms sector. However, this candidate displayed exceptional ability, had a great track record with a well rounded and dynamic personality. I worked with the candidate and identified an employer that had a great culture where I felt she would excel. I had considerable confidence in her and recommended she should be considered for the role. The potential employer agreed but felt her CV lacked the industry experience of the other three shortlisted candidates.

I had belief in this candidate and requested her application was put on hold rather than be rejected. Whilst the remaining candidates displayed excellent experience and had the requisite skills, none met the cultural fit of the company and so were rejected. I put the candidate forward confidently for interview. She studiously researched the brand and her creative approach displayed how she could add considerable value. Her initiative and exceptionally well rounded, dynamic and entrepreneurial character was identified by my employer. She was offered the position and successfully moved to the telecoms sector.

For further insights and proven methods that give you an unfair advantage in the current job market, visit www.beajobmagnet.co.uk

Your time is now - Choice in the intelligence age

Tony Buzan (2010), the creator of mind maps, suggests that we are no longer in the information age but have moved to the intelligence age. We are constantly subjected to endless information, both at work and at home. To be successful in this intelligence age you have to be effective at filtering the information you need. By utilising the latest technologies, combined with the clarity of your chosen career pathway, you will be able to identify the relevant information thus avoiding overload. Creating compelling goals for your career will provide this direction and this topic will be covered in the next chapter.

1

ACTION POINTS

1. Identify your key 5 strengths - what are you good at? What do people say you do naturally well?

_____

_____

_____

_____

_____

2. Identify what motivates you and what you are passionate about.

_____

_____

_____

_____

_____

3. Acknowledge your career dreams.

_____

_____

_____

1

4. Document your career successes and failures to date. Ask
yourself what you have learnt from them.

5. Take the time to clarify what your 'A' game would be and start to
work out how you could play that every day.

6. Identify what are the most significant industries and careers that
you believe will present the greatest opportunities for you in the
next decade.

1

7. How can you believe in yourself more? Wherever you are at this current time, you have got huge resources and potential that you could share with others.

8. Commit to being remarkable; document 5 actions that would make you remarkable - the very best version of yourself! Don't try to be someone else, everybody else is taken!

Secret 2

How to create momentum and achieve your 'ideal career' goals

Having gained clarity on your strengths, goal setting will enable you to focus on the appropriate actions to achieve your ideal career. By setting stretch goals in your career, you are asking your mind to search out resources that will allow you to achieve those goals; the alternative is to wait for career opportunities to be created for you.

2

By setting short, medium and long term goals you will be able to take control of your career; this in turn has a fundamental impact on the fulfilment and happiness of your life. All of life's successful achievers set goals and work towards them. This is true in every field of success e.g. business, sport, art. Part of the pleasure of this process is ticking off the goals when they have been achieved.

At interview, many have given vague answers when questioned about their career goals for the next five years. Be different, take the time and visualise your ideal job and career pathway 1 year from now, 3 years from now and in 5 to 10 years' time; this starts the process and creates momentum.

We tend to overestimate what we can achieve in a year and underestimate what we can achieve in a lifetime. So setting some frankly unrealistic goals relative to where you are today over the long term is exactly what all high achievers do. Having clarified where you want to be, you will begin to attract the resources into your life that will allow you to move towards your goals, see more opportunities and join the dots together.

It is important to break down these seemingly huge tasks into smaller steps and keep asking yourself what step I need to take next. Complete the step and move onto the next step systematically. Being persistent and patient is fundamental to ultimately achieving your ideal career. Just as importantly, your focus will enable you to say no to certain demands ensuring that you utilise your most precious gifts, time and energy effectively.

The most valuable exercise of my career

I had reached a point in my career where I felt that I wanted to examine how I could develop and become more successful. My first step was to identify and subsequently interview ten people who had achieved the results that I desired. These leaders were all very successful in their chosen fields and, as a result, very wealthy, in some cases millionaires.

I wanted to uncover what had made them successful. They were from a variety of disciplines which included property development, technology and accountancy. I considered all of these people to be super successful in their chosen field. I was very nervous about making contact with them and wondered if they would help me; however the result was fascinating. By stepping out of my network, making a friendly introduction and acknowledging their successes, every one of them was willing to share their wisdom and career story.

The very first theme that became apparent was that these individuals had a clear understanding of long term gain. One individual had moved to the Thames Valley and was unable to afford his own property. He visualised an image of his ideal home and identified what he would need to do to achieve it. He then broke this down to manageable steps and scaled it back to where he currently was. This goal was way beyond his current circumstance but he knew why he wanted to do it. His motivation was fuelled by his desire to provide for his children and family. Identifying why you want to achieve a particular goal is fundamental to its achievement. Suffice to say he now lives in his beautiful ideal home and owns many other properties.

These individuals also all had a very strong action orientation. That is they didn't wait around for the perfect conditions, they started their undertaking regardless. They learnt from any mistakes and developed their action in response. Critically, all of them were very confident that even with the inevitable obstacles they would eventually achieve their goals or even exceed them.

2

When they came up against setbacks or a recession, they adjusted their behaviour accordingly and continued to see these 'opportunities' as part of the journey. They also continually invested in themselves, developing greater knowledge and skills. One of them who is now in his sixties described to me how he still actively seeks new knowledge. He learns from every experience and then applies that new knowledge daily in his business career. With such an approach it is no wonder that he is hugely successful.

I learnt that if they can achieve amazing career goals, so can I and, in turn, you - so we must Evolve, Implement and Achieve!

For further insights and proven methods that give you an unfair advantage in the current job market, visit www.beajobmagnet.co.uk

So how do you gain clarity on your career goals?

There are some fortunate people who seem to gain total clarity very early on in their careers about which path they will take. A number of years ago I met a Director of a high profile business who said that at the age of 25 he had already made the decision and knew precisely where his career was going. He was going to be the Managing Director of the company. This focus/clarity ensured that every daily thought, action and interaction he made moved him towards that goal.

So how can this clarity help you achieve your ideal career?

Having a strong connection with that ideal career is a great place to start, combined with your belief that the goal is stretching yet achievable for you. Below are the critical steps I have observed that allow successful people to craft their ideal career moves.

Visualisation

I know many of you may question the merit of visualisation when planning your ideal career pathway but please bear with me. All of us paint images in our mind daily and all I am asking you to do is perceive those images as positive and empowering for your life.

You need to visualise your ideal business day and connect with the images and actions that will produce a positive and effective day for you. Set it as your goal with the intention to achieve this day consistently. Most successful businessmen and women utilise it very productively. Recently I had the pleasure to meet Sue Stone, a business and confidence coach, as seen on the TV series 'The Secret Millionaire' (2011).

She shared with me some of the techniques she used to transform her life, one of the most empowering being visualisation. At least three times a day she visualises her goals as completed events and focuses on how this will make her feel, what she will see, hear and how she will talk to herself. She also constantly checks in with herself to reframe any negative or non empowering thoughts into a positive one that will move her towards her goals.

How to visualise your goals:

- Focus on what you do want. Use what you don't want as a catalyst for what you do.

- Have a positive attitude to the meaning of events and challenges that occur along the way to achieving your goals. Seek to learn from each situation thus enabling you to move towards your goal.

- Use the lessons learnt to adapt your behaviour and be flexible for the next situation you find yourself in.

2

- When you are facing a challenging situation, assess your success from the past and remind yourself of recent achievements and contributions you have made. This will put you in a very positive and confident frame of mind as you move towards your ideal career.

- View the achievement of your next career move as a process, visualise each step and enjoy the process, take daily actions towards it and seek 'progress' rather than perfection.

In summary you need to Evolve into the person you desire, Implement the actions of that person and then you will Achieve the benefits and rewards such people in their ideal careers have.

Your connection to your career goals

I realised a number of years ago that when people have set goals for me, I was creating someone else's dream and I was lacking the ownership of the attainment of the goal because they were not my own. The important thing to do is to have ownership of the goal, you created it and you have a huge compelling reason why you want to achieve it.

For example, if you want to be a Director and you need to improve your influencing/leadership skills or your communication skills, start today and investigate the opportunity of leading training courses that will enable you to improve those skills. Another option is to identify people that you admire as leaders and connect with them and begin to learn from them. Persist with this process and your success will be inevitable.

Taking ownership for your career goals – the successes and the failures

One of the most valuable lessons I have learnt is from Jack Canfield, a world leading authority on success. His book entitled 'The Success Principles' (2005) is widely considered as the bible of how to be successful. Jack identifies that we must take 100% responsibility for our life and in turn our results.

The important distinction is about taking responsibility so that you are 'response-able', in other words you have the ability to respond to an event rather than blaming yourself or anybody else. You actually take responsibility for everything you have done, both the successes and the failures. This isn't about giving yourself a hard time but it is about accepting where you are and asking how you created that result in your life, so you can adjust your behaviours and move forward. Remember how you respond to an event will determine the outcome, both positive and negative.

This is clearly demonstrated in the following example where two of my candidates responded to the recent recession in very different ways.

Candidate A, who we will call Harold, and Candidate B, who we will call Michael, were relatively evenly matched in terms of skill set and experience. Both candidates had been made redundant from their organisations.

Harold had a strong career to date and had been headhunted regularly throughout his career; this meant he had never really focused on searching for his next career option. Having been made redundant he started to search for job opportunities and he quickly realised that they were few and far between, however he was optimistic that opportunities would present themselves to him. I suggested some potential avenues for him to explore including how to network effectively and really try to get him to take responsibility for his next actions.

When I spoke with him at a later date he reported that everything was somebody else's fault, it was the credit crunch, employers not returning calls, people not wanting to network, it was everybody else's fault. This resulted in him almost at one point being quite depressed with the whole situation.

In contrast, Michael had a completely different attitude. In the first instance, he just said "Redundancy - it happens, it has happened to other people, I am determined to find my next position." This candidate probably had slightly less experience but he was absolutely determined to achieve his goal, and he was also very flexible in terms of how he was going to achieve it. Of course he had knock backs, he was getting to second stage, to final stage and then the job was being withdrawn but he just kept persevering - he had that resilience!

Eventually he decided to take a temporary position and over a couple of months he got a new opportunity which led him to achieving his ideal permanent role. The secret to his success was that he kept his spirits high, and viewed the whole process as a challenge that would equip him better for the future.

Harold did eventually get a job but it took nearly a year and this caused him a huge amount of stress. This really illustrates the difference one's attitude can make. As I say, Harold probably had a stronger background, but it is those grumbles, fears and frustrations that we give into every day that don't allow us to be released and in turn effective.

For further insights and proven methods that give you an unfair advantage in the current job market, visit www.beajobmagnet.co.uk

2

CASE STUDY
How to demonstrate your potential...

Preparation and planning prevents a poor performance. An individual within my network contacted me looking for his next career move. He wanted to work for an innovative technology company. I considered all of the technology employers and thought that one in particular would be an excellent match.

The company in question agreed with my recommendation. They interviewed my candidate but unfortunately appointed internally. There was, however, a strong connection between the company and my candidate. I stayed in touch with him and twelve months later a new opportunity arose with the same company. The role was outside of the candidate's key skill sets but he had significant initiative, a proven track record and exceptional future potential.

My candidate was yet again up against an internal candidate with a strong reputation who had excellent experience within a particular technology. As my candidate had limited experience within this particular technology I decided to meet with the recruiting team to gain a thorough understanding of the criteria they would use in appraising each applicant. A key criterion was that candidates had to display 'exceptional future potential'. I was confident in my candidate's ability so we prepared a plan to demonstrate his potential. He was successful in his final interview and was offered the role. He is doing a great job and is advancing his career.

Setting yourself up for career success

When you have set your ideal career goals you must maintain flexibility in your plan to achieve them, and be realistic. Accept where you are currently and concentrate fully on the next important action and be persistent.

I got this wrong initially when I started career goal setting. I got frustrated because I didn't achieve my desired results instantly. I didn't want to wait years! This is a sure way to unhappiness. The whole point of goals is that they give you a vision for an exciting and compelling future. They require a workable plan and then consistent action in small manageable pieces. Reference back to our Managing Director, it took him 10 years to achieve that position but he achieved his goal and enjoyed the journey.

Creating the best version possible of yourself is the key to achieving your career goals. This area is covered in the next chapter which explores you as a brand.

ACTION  POINTS

1. Write down your seemingly unachievable greatest ambitions in your career.

_____

_____

_____

_____

_____

2. Identify people that have achieved the career results you desire. Spend time with them, asking questions but more importantly listening. Make a connection with them; this could be the most valuable relationship you ever create. What are the important distinctions that have made them successful?

_____

_____

_____

_____

_____

3. What will enable you to commit to spending time each week on your specific career goal and actions? When you have completed that goal, visualise how you will feel, what you will see and hear and what you will say to yourself.

2

_____

_____

_____

_____

_____

4. Commit to acting upon inspired ideas to create momentum towards your ideal career. What inspired ideas have you recently had?

_____

_____

_____

_____

_____

5. How can you be the person you desire to be? How can you implement the behaviours of that person and enjoy achieving the rewards?

_____

_____

_____

_____

_____

6. Realise that you are going to face challenges. Ask yourself how you are going to respond to these challenges moving you closer to your desired career.

_____

_____

_____

_____

_____

2

2

Secret 3

How to create the most valuable brand in your life!

Have you ever wondered why it is that certain people can earn so much more than others? Within our careers we are all searching to add more value to ourselves and to others whilst being well rewarded for it. To achieve this it is fundamental to develop your own distinctive high value brand as an employee.

Naturally results are a key component and I believe coupled with these is the overriding factor of perceived value - just like why we pay more for an iPhone rather than any other smartphone. Perceived value is the most important criteria when buying products and in my experience employers follow this pattern too. I am assuming that by choosing this book you have produced some good results and you are accomplished at what you do but your career isn't at the stage you would like.

Business guru Tom Peters developed the concept of 'Brand you' (2009). He identified branding as really giving yourself every opportunity to succeed in your chosen area and to proactively take charge of your career choices. This has never been more relevant than it is today.

What is your own brand?

I believe your own brand has three key components:

• Your reputation and what you stand for

• Your integrity (do you do what you say you are going to do?)

• Skills you have mastered – value you offer

When these three factors mirror what employers' value, you are on your way to achieving that elusive state - your ideal career.

The good news is that you are in control of what career choices you have. The challenging news is that you will be paid on how potential employers perceive your value; your career acceleration will depend on this.

This chapter focuses on how to increase your perceived value and then in turn be appropriately rewarded for the value you have added to your future employers. Critically you need to understand yourself, have nurtured your passion and purpose and have clarity of your real strengths. You must master your functional specialism and develop a clearly defined and unique proposition that makes you stand out in the job market adding significant value to employers on an on-going basis. Enhancing your brand is also about building awareness.

Getting your face wet to build awareness of your message/brand

First let me share with you a story from a book I have been fortunate enough to be reading entitled 'Achieving the Impossible' written by Lewis Pugh (2010). Lewis is an explorer, an athlete and an inspiration. He is passionate about raising awareness and stopping the destruction of planet earth.

3

He is a very good swimmer (his strength) and he has an innate ability to swim in temperatures that would normally kill many other people. He became the first person to swim across the North Pole and then not content with that he actually swam across the South Pole! This is an extreme example of building your brand message and one which has given him a lot of media coverage. This has resulted in Lewis being given the opportunity to express his concerns to influential individuals like Tony Blair and Prince Charles on environmental change.

This is an example which clearly demonstrates that if you are passionate enough about something, you use your strengths and you do something a bit different to get the platform you need to share your message and influence key decision makers effectively.

As an employee it is really important for us to be very mindful as to what our brand represents not only in terms of value set etc, but also how we build our reputation as experts in our own particular area of expertise. I believe you can never start that too early. The world's most successful people build their brand, their knowledge and their expertise in a never ending cycle of success and enhancement.

Using your brand to attract opportunities

Commit to being excellent in your chosen field of expertise and then amplify your message by becoming a 'Brand' in your own right.

So how do you build your brand? – My 8 Step success formula

Step 1: Your online CV

Having a strong LinkedIn profile is very important in today's market. Like many of today's headhunters one of my first sources of candidates is LinkedIn. Ensuring that your LinkedIn profile is up to date with a key focus on your areas of expertise, achievements and areas of responsibility makes you visible – this is your marketing brochure. Ultimately it is very similar to your CV so it should be written in a very similar professional manner. A selective number of recommendations from people who are in a position to comment on the value you have added provides evidence of your abilities and attitudes.

Previous line mangers, peer groups, clients or customer are all valuable sources. I would encourage you to aim to have 10 key quality recommendations and you will enjoy the reflected light by being associated with high profile individuals.

From the offline perspective, keep yourself and your CV up to date every three months irrespective of whether you are actively looking to change job. Not only does this remind you of your successes to date, but also ensures you are prepared if an opportunity arises.

3

Step 2: Utilise social media for your business purpose

One of the most important things is to examine yourself and develop an effective presence within the online community. Naturally Facebook and Twitter can be used exclusively for business, promoting yourself as an expert in your chosen field. You can comment on and solve problems for people both within and outside your industry, becoming known as a person who gives and adds value.

Step 3: Having your own blog

Developing a blog, where you share your knowledge and key insights, is a natural step to building your authority and credibility within any industry. Having your own website and your own YouTube channel are certainly potential areas to develop so that your profile is raised and people can start to build trust with you. This can take a bit of time and requires some effort, but the aim is to craft and create yourself as the expert and authority within your field.

For further insights and proven methods that give you an unfair advantage in the current job market, visit www.beajobmagnet.co.uk

Step 4: Join industry groups

Collaboration works!! Join relevant groups within your industry, both online and offline, ensuring that you participate in relevant discussions and forums. There are many groups that aren't relevant, so focus on the ones that are really going to add value to your particular area.

Online professional networks are also a great resource when looking for jobs. There are more and more employers proactively looking to target this 'unadvertised candidate' market. You can identify which companies are recruiting, go onto the company jobsite and identify who the recruiting manager and often the line manager is. You can then link with an individual you know at the targeted company and facilitate yourself a warm introduction.

Step 5: Develop a leader's and influencer's mindset

You can call it your 'leader's mindset'. If you identify that your line manager or other influential people within your organisation have a business problem, try and offer to help them, even if it is in a small way, because these things do come back. I recently met an individual who I had given interview advice to in the past. He had since moved to another recruitment company and was contacting me with an opportunity of a job that needed to be filled. So my one good turn came back and I actually benefitted from it. It is absolutely critical to take all opportunities presented and be seen as the go to person in your field.

Step 6: Speak publicly - it's win-win!

An ideal way to build your profile and your brand is to speak at events. As soon as you walk on stage you are assumed to be an authority. Naturally you need to be able to deliver value to your audience. Most individuals don't take this step because they don't believe they know enough and it's only for gurus. I know that you will have knowledge that will add value to people and by sharing it you will help others and also raise your own profile.

Step 7: Invest in yourself

This is a real passion of mine. Constantly investing in yourself, exposing yourself to new ideas and new people really drives your development forward. In the words of Jim Rohn (2011), "A formal education will make you a living; self education will make you a fortune."

Every year I commit myself to develop four new habits that will propel me forward over the coming year. Recently I focused on developing my communication, speaking skills, my influencing and leadership skills; this has not been easy but hugely productive. You may also find this a challenge as you will need to move outside your comfort zone almost by definition.

Talent alone is not enough to reach your career potential

People at the very top of their profession consistently listen to advice to continually improve. They focus on deliberate action plans which will enhance their strengths and improve their weaknesses.

In a later chapter I have identified the key skills that senior level board members value in their organisations e.g. being a key influencer in the organisation and being innovative. I urge you to deliberately target one at a time and seek to improve your skill and application of such valuable skills.

I recently read an article on Placido Domingo (Zanartu 2010), the greatest living tenor. He describes his mind as a parachute that is most effective when open. He refers to an incident where after a particular performance a voice coach gave him some specific feedback that there was part of his delivery that could be improved. This was a brave voice coach! Low and behold, Domingo was back in the following morning a couple of hours before rehearsals on the piano refining his performance. If you want to get ahead in your career and your market, make yourself more valuable. Invest in yourself.

Fill your mind with positivity and possibility

3

We are bombarded with bad news. I have given up reading newspapers – I only read the business, culture and appointments sections. You are going to get depressed if you listen to the 10 o'clock news every night and take that to bed with you. I make it a commitment of mine every evening to go to bed with positivity, looking at the goals I want to achieve in the future.

Step 8: Learn from and join the top 10% in your industry

A fast tracked route to building your brand is to learn from and join the top 10% in your industry. Here's how -

1: Identify the top 10% of people in your industry.

2: Develop a plan of how to connect with those individuals.

3: Connect with them – here is an example of how I did it.

I was looking to connect with Jeff Grout who had previously been the Managing Director for a market leading recruitment company and had made the successful transition to bestselling author and advisor to high performance business and sporting teams including the world cup winning 2003 England rugby team.

Below are the precise words I used to connect with him and gain a very valuable half an hour of his time, to ask him 5 key questions surrounding his success.

"Hello Jeff, my name is Adrian Evans. We have not met yet. I know you are a busy man, so I will be brief. I own my own Search & Selection business. Over the years you have done an excellent job of building the Robert Half business and moving into the public speaking and coaching arena. I have read and enjoyed a number of your books including 'Mind Games' (2004). I am sure you had many challenges when you were first starting out. I am still at those early stages, trying to figure out everything. Jeff, I would really appreciate if you would spend half hour of your time to answer a few questions."

This resulted in a very successful conversation for me.

4: Develop your unique brand pitch and proposition of value added skills and results.

5: Identify the top trends in your industry and prepare plans that solve key decision makers' business problems.

6: Interview and act like the top 10%. Achievers expect to achieve their goals and fully believe they deserve them

7: Persist until your desired results are achieved.

This process will enable you to develop into the go to person and an authority within your industry.

For further insights and proven methods that give you an unfair advantage in the current job market, visit www.beajobmagnet.co.uk

You will need to have specific mentors who will accelerate your development in key skill areas such as influence, innovation and assured confidence. The way to approach mentors is outlined above. Identify people who have achieved the results you desire; ask them if you could have a short amount of their time to ask how they achieved their results. Some of these contacts will be a one-off conversation; many could turn into an on-going and mutually beneficial relationships. Keynote here is to always thank mentors for their valuable time invested in you, offer to assist them in any way you can, follow their advice and keep them up to date with your progress if they desire.

Read relevant books, subscribe to magazines/blogs relevant to your industry as well as connecting with people who are going to help you move forward. Go to seminars! I recently attended a multi-day seminar which led to some significant rethinks and breakthroughs for me. I realised huge possibilities and now invest at least 5 days a year attending seminars.

I invest at least an hour a day on personal development and continue to improve my game. This is how you are going to get to the top. This is what people who do get there do; they don't let things stand in their way. There is no doubt, that speaking publically and becoming an industry expert is the difference between those that stay as functional experts and those who move to the next level.

Speaking from a platform to an audience is one of the single biggest ways of improving your communication skills, and the great bonus is that you get your message out to a far bigger audience, and not just one to one. You build your brand and there is a golden line that as you step on stage you become an expert and your credibility increases. It also allows you to communicate effectively and build your confidence.

Public speaking can be scary so start on a subject you have earned the right to talk about and one that you are passionate about. I have found that when that happens the words and your passion shine, and it seems to go well.

Currently, one of the best communicators on the planet, Barack Obama, happens to be one of the most powerful leaders on the planet as well. America has transformed its reputation in the last few years because of him, and a lot of that is down to communication. Every reason to focus on speaking.

I recommend you commit to spending a small fixed percentage of your annual income on your professional self development – you will never get a return on investment like it! You are investing in you – you will always get a return back on that.

3

In summary no matter where you are in your career at present I truly believe you deserve to have the opportunity to express your skills every day and have your ideal career. The tools provided so far in the book will allow you to calmly and confidently grow into that situation. I know some people will not use these tools and they will not gain the positive outcomes I have identified. I urge you to work with these tools and take yourself to the next level in your career. I believe you can move to being the very best version of yourself and be appropriately rewarded.

ACTION **POINTS**

1. What is your unique pitch/value proposition? Rehearse your unique pitch/value proposition to network with the top 10% of contacts in your chosen industry.

_____

_____

_____

_____

_____

2. Seek out and attract public speaking opportunities within your industry/organisation and socially – it's a great confidence builder. Which opportunities spring to mind?

_____

_____

_____

_____

_____

3. Formalise your knowledge by writing it down. Think about what expertise people seek from you.

_____

_____

4. Develop your business social media profile. How can you enhance your LinkedIn profile?

5. Identify which 4 key skills will accelerate your career forward and focus on those one at a time.

6. Commit to implementing at least 3 action points from every book you read, training course/webinar you attend and coaching session you are part of. Which 3 points could you implement today that would make a difference to your career?

3

The ultimate **career** development toolkit

Secret 4

How to access the 'hidden' job market and grow your career faster than ever before.

A critical element of any effective career strategy is networking and where the value can really be multiplied is by developing a targeted networking plan. Ultimately this will have a direct impact on your mindset, your knowledge, your career opportunities, your wealth and your prospects in life.

It is not a 'dark art' or something you should be overly nervous about – we all network in our everyday lives to some degree or another without giving it a title of networking, but what we are talking about here is the structured style of networking that will accelerate your job search success and your career.

The fundamental result of effective networking is the exposure to others who have already achieved what you are aiming to achieve. In modelling these successful individuals, initially by adopting their approach and applying their techniques, you will actually realise your goals and full potential. Clearly effective networking is a critical skill one needs to achieve career success.

Why network?

Ultimately what you are aiming to achieve is to connect with people who are going to leverage your career. I believe leverage is the key that multiplies the effect of the effort and time that you are actually putting in. It is widely recognised that Archimedes boldly claimed that if he had a lever long enough he could move the world. This concept applies so well to networking. It is a great way of leveraging knowledge and people to achieve your goal and to accelerate your career, your promotion, or your level of earnings to the next level. It is in your interests to do so.

The successful people in this world don't question how I can get more time, (we all have 24 hours a day, 365 days a year) they seek to leverage this valuable resource taking it forward. The internet has developed as one of the most useful tools in utilising one's time effectively. It enables us to acquire knowledge quickly and develop it further which is absolutely critical.

I truly believe that your networks are your net worth. In other words the depth and calibre of the individuals within your network can increase your potential both personally and financially. Many of us are familiar with the concept of the six degrees of separation. That is that we are all connected through a maximum of five acquaintances. This is truly remarkable, however I would like to term it the six degrees of success. The reason being that you will usually discover that the person you really need to talk to is only two/three/four degrees away from you and as such so is your success.

Networking also opens up the hidden job market. I would still say most job opportunities are actually sourced via people's network, and that is coming from a headhunter. When I initially start working with a client I begin by identifying where they are with the candidate search. Every line manager states that they have looked internally and have also explored their network in an attempt to identify anybody who is right for the role. This is the very first thing they do. They don't put an advert in the press or online; they think who else within my network could fulfil this role.

4

What is networking and how do we do it?

I perceive networking as the development of relationships that are positive and productive for all involved. Many recognise that in the exchanging of information and pooling of resources, effective networks can improve productivity and thus improve working lives. The most effective business development tool for networking is to develop relationships before you need them.

Also consider the power of your network's network. I was recently researching information on growing my business and the ten people I eventually approached about this were just outside my network, but literally just outside. With the power of your network's network suddenly you can move from 200 individuals, who you could possibly tap into, to potentially thousands of people. Look at your LinkedIn network and how many people this ultimately links you to, via your connections – it's astounding.

Let us look at the cause and effect of networking. This is clearly demonstrated when the time comes to look for a career change. Imagine that you haven't developed a particularly strong network and when it comes to looking for a job, 'the effect' is that you end up struggling and not utilising your precious time effectively. If however, you have already developed strong foundations and have an effective network of people to tap into, they could help by putting you in contact with either their own businesses or other helpful contacts.

The following example clearly demonstrates the positive benefits of effective networking.

4

I was approached recently by an interior designer who was about to launch a new book on a topic that she thought I might have some expertise in, this being small business owners and what their needs were when trying to expand their business. She was keen to understand how important it was for them to get the most energy and productivity out of their environment. I gave her a number of ideas on the key issues that many small business owners face in terms of organising their days and being productive and getting results.

I was happy to do this because what I received in return was a number of proven ideas about how to launch a book and how to gain publicity and this was from a published author. Ultimately we have the start of a mutually beneficial trusting responsive relationship that is going to evolve over a period of time where both parties give and receive as a direct result. My advice is to go into networking appropriately, equipped with your best manners and best intentions. You must also have a giving mindset in that you must first give significant value in order to receive.

How to network for career success – The proven WIN/WIN networking formula

4

Which 10 people if I networked with would accelerate my career most rapidly?

Identify how you can help this person in their professional or personal life.

Now be flexible.

When connecting with people, be completely present.

Integrate social networking into your networking strategy.

Network online with the same integrity and approach as offline.

You need to ask yourself the following:

1. Which 10 people if I networked with would accelerate my career most rapidly?

I cannot emphasise enough that even if you are not looking for a new role in the immediate future, it is vitally important to be building relationships and networking every month, digging your well before you require the water so to speak. If you are actively looking for a role, you probably want to increase that number quite significantly to 50.

For further insights and proven methods that give you an unfair advantage in the current job market, visit www.beajobmagnet.co.uk

The next key issue to address is to:

2. Identify how you can help this person in their professional or personal life

Identify what business they are in; you may be able to establish if there is a business opportunity you could put their way as a lead or as a follow up. Expect nothing in return and you are detached from any results. Remember networking is about giving, giving and hopefully receiving some returned value at some point in the future.

Formulate this list and plan your approach. You don't want to suddenly ask for a lot of peoples' time, time is one of our most valuable commodities. Start with email; start with short telephone conversations spending 80% of the conversation on the key 20% of advice that is going to give you the results you want. You need to persist to see whether your tactics are actually working.

3. Now be flexible

If you don't think this approach is working for you, refine it. Start from a place where you believe you are worthy and you can gain and pass information that will have a positive impact. Utilise anything and everything to your advantage.

Dale Carnegie probably said it best when he said "Talk in terms of other person's interests" (1936). When you are actually talking to somebody, be engaged and think about what interests them rather than just talking about you. Whenever you meet somebody, and I mean anybody irrespective of their role, believe that you are equal to them. This ensures that you won't get 'star-struck' or on the other hand talk down to people. The critical thing is that when you meet people, treat people with respect and as peers. When I started taking this attitude, a lot more doors opened for me.

4. When connecting with people, be completely present

Try and give your complete attention to that person, don't focus on anything else, be with that person completely. When you actually meet somebody, don't think of them just as an individual, think of them as a representative of all the people they know and all the people that those people know.

Give the best representation of everything you do and how you conduct yourself. This ensures that you really promote yourself effectively as a brand. Of the people you talk to, 20% will give you 80% of the results, so of 10 conversations you have 2 of them will be absolute pearls that you take forward and develop productive reciprocal relationships.

5. Integrate social networking into your networking strategy

For me this is a hugely important tool in the networking process. Facebook, LinkedIn and Twitter continue to develop at an exponential rate. As a headhunter I am constantly logged onto LinkedIn every single day. It is the most valuable tool and my way of identifying new candidates, new job opportunities, keeping abreast of news and content and ultimately connecting with individuals in the marketplace. The key reasons why I favour LinkedIn are that they already have over 6 million members in the UK, over 100 million globally, and half of the FTSE 100 companies now hire through LinkedIn, as do 50% of the Fortune 100. For me it is business focused, it is professional in both its outlook and focus. Interestingly it has been reported that they are looking to develop their proposition as a job website.

This is further supported by companies like Microsoft who have identified LinkedIn to make significant recruitment savings; also Accenture plans to recruit 50,000 staff including telecoms consultants, finance experts and software specialists using LinkedIn. It is evident that LinkedIn is highly valuable in any career search.

6. Network online with the same integrity and approach as offline

There are some golden rules when it comes to utilising online networks, the same rules apply online as they do offline. If you are trying to connect with people and network effectively, be polite and courteous. People often forget that when they are social networking, they are not talking to a computer, they are talking to another person. One must consider how the communication is actually going to be received. Think about the individual and whether you would connect with them offline, if so then that is a good idea to connect with them online.

CASE STUDY
How networking achieved 3 job offers during the worse recession since the 1930s

To illustrate the power of a deliberate and strategic approach to networking I have outlined a real life example of how a very proactive candidate gained three offers and secured his ultimate career move during the depths of the recession.

This candidate had a very successful career track record and the difference that made the difference was in his approach.

He deliberately planned his next career move. He was clear he wanted to work in a very specific culture that would provide the right environment to advance his career. He took time to understand his key motivations and career pathway, so the brainstorming phase was set in motion as all sectors and potential organisations were considered.

4

This is something all of us can do. When I spoke with him at the time there was a calm, considered confidence and certainty that he could achieve a number of offers in a relatively short period of time during a difficult recruitment market. Over the next few weeks the plan evolved and he started to add filters that would refine the search. He looked at which actual companies and categories he wanted to be in. He not only considered salary and location, but also social purpose and striking a work life balance. He came to a significant discovery; he felt he would thrive in a medium sized organisation with greater scope for progression rather than a major corporate.

Having completed his plan he set about the action phase. He contacted all the relevant people he knew – he was lifting the rocks to find out more about organisations, cultures and possibilities. This started with simple 5 minute conversations, that resulted in 2 or 3 further contacts being created and so his network grew. He also developed his interested in Micro Finance, an area he was passionate about and one where he felt he could give back.

After the initial conversations the interesting opportunities became more in depth and a winning loop was established. All the conversations were specifically followed up with emails, followed by face to face meetings. He ensured that he kept momentum by recording all activity on a spreadsheet. From this he developed a research base. At the beginning and end of the day he started to explore opportunities, updated his LinkedIn profile, and produced a compelling and achievement led CV. He started to see himself as a brand and a service to take to market. He took a step by step approach, breaking the process down into which organisations he was going to contact directly, who he was going to network with, cold call, and which recruitment companies could assist his search.

He very quickly came to the conclusion that his time was best spent networking to create more opportunities. His LinkedIn contacts grew from 120 to in excess of 500 contacts over just a couple of months. He felt this was a very natural and collaborative approach.

4

He wrote his plan down and actually gave himself some targets. How many calls per week? How many face to face meetings? At the same time he still had a day job and he needed to create about 10 extra hours a week. He did this by just getting up earlier and working in the evening. The coffee house became his third home, but it gave him dedicated time to focus on what he was looking to achieve. His mindset was right and he formed a clear goal.

He had the full support of his wife and family. He was the CEO of the 'family' and his wife was the Chairman. This emotional support was critical.

Using this **collaborative win/win approach** he secured interviews with a number of companies, he was able to demonstrate value to three organisations that were keen to employ him. In some of the cases there wasn't a job, it didn't exist but he created one to his requirements. He achieved this by taking the approach of "What can I do to help you?"

One of the companies did stand out. They had a unique and very dynamic culture which the candidate felt he could thrive in; he accepted their offer as a VP and was able to leave his existing employer on mutually agreeable terms. This real life example clearly demonstrates that even in a challenging market a detailed networking plan backed up by appropriate action can lead you to achieve your desired outcome.

It is interesting to note that the candidate felt in control of the process, he has ended up in an ideal role that he believes has been collaboratively created. During the process he extended his network. Even the roles he turned down he conducted himself appropriately and was able to enhance his reputation.

4

Summary of case study

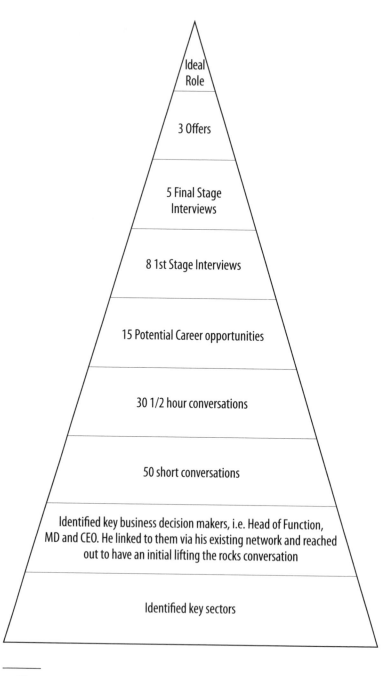

4

I believe this is a winning formula for anyone seeking a career move in any market

For further insights and proven methods that give you an unfair advantage in the current job market, visit www.beajobmagnet.co.uk

CONCLUSION

Successful people network deliberately with clear goals established.

Whilst 'social networking' is a modern term, networking is one of the oldest and most useful skills you can possibly have. Start with the end in mind, if you truly want to be successful in networking, ultimately your dominant thoughts will determine your actions and your actions will determine your results.

4

ACTION  POINTS

1. Below, identify 10 people that you could network with to accelerate your career the most.

How to effectively identify the people you want to work with

You ultimately need to identify the key people who are going to make all the difference. This is niche marketing rather than mass marketing. I would use the following criteria:

a) **Influence**: what ability or authority does this person have - either their personal position or their ability to be able to influence your career. Having clarity and being clear on what industry you want to be in is critical.

b) **Profile**: are they recognised already as a role model and as an aspirational leader?

c) **Potential**: what potential has this person to have a significant impact on their particular industry over the next few years, will their authority and responsibility grow?

2. Write out a short script and contact these people.

3. Dedicate at least three hours a month to actively network and make new connections and associations. (Toastmasters, industry forums etc). Which event are you going to next?

4

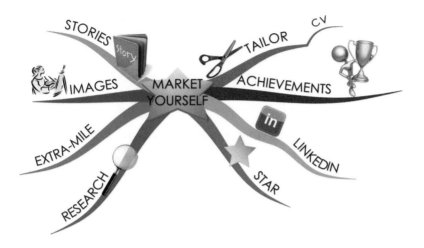

Secret 5

How to market yourself

Being ready for when opportunities knock!

As the recruiting process has evolved extensively over the last few decades, you may ask why is it important to have a great CV and be able to present yourself effectively at interview.

Most employers will start your application with a request for a well constructed CV. If they then wish to explore how close the match is to their culture and the job fit, a series of interviews is still the most popular method. Often a presentation or some additional psychometric testing may be included within this process.

Your CV is your marketing message to potential employers

Based on my extensive experience and research in this area I would urge you to view constructing a compelling CV as both science and art. It requires an appropriate structure, tangibility and an opportunity for your style, personality and approach to shine.

What is the purpose of your CV?

Your CV exists with the sole purpose of getting you an initial interview. Your CV may be your first and only opportunity to make an impression on a potential employer. Make sure that it is a compelling first impression and creates a positive impact, inciting sufficient interest to warrant an interview so they want to find out more about you.

Key considerations when writing your CV

This is a subject we discuss at our teleseminars and workshops at great length, and with these key points you will be well on the way to securing yourself an interview. One question I always ask people to ask themselves, is your CV the best possible version of you?

Do's

- Tailor your CV to the specific role that you're applying for as it will highlight the areas of your experience that are most

5

relevant to the role, thus giving a greater likelihood of being invited in for an interview to showcase yourself in person.

- Use keywords in your CV; it will make it easier for employers and recruiters to find you on internet searches – therefore including terms that are relevant to the role you are seeking are critical to help you to be tracked down.

- Refresh/upload your CV onto the job boards that you use every week. This ensures that it is one of the first profiles seen when agencies/companies search.

- Ensure you identify your career goals as this displays ambition and clarity of purpose by yourself.

- If you are going to include a profile, ensure that it is action orientated and that it includes results with data. For instance, "I am a strategic leader with a track record of X and Y," you can then include some tangible results. Whenever you can, quantify your results. Numbers can serve to illustrate your degree of success or level of authority and responsibility very effectively.

5

- Make sure your CV is accurate and leave no unexplained gaps.

- Use the funnel approach. Begin with the organisation, then the division you are currently working within and finally your role. If it is a large business, include the dimensions i.e. turnover, products, services and customers. Follow on with just four or five bullet points per previous job starting with action words.

- Make sure that your CV emphasises both the context and content of your responsibilities and achievements, strengths and successes. Whenever possible, use positive action words, for example: 'led', 'created', 'launched', 'developed', 'achieved', 'improved', 'negotiated', 'managed' and 'on time and under budget'. This demonstrates measurable results and, if there is not a level of confidentiality attached to these achievements, put them in.

- Include your education; your highest level of education. Also include any training or continued development you have invested in yourself. Whether that be personal development courses, leadership courses or communication skills. These are the key areas that we are really looking to demonstrate to people.

- To be successful, it is imperative that the key decision makers are exposed to your CV. If you are rejected by anyone other than this person, persist and find a route to them.

- Use the Internet to Enhance your Career Search:

  i. LinkedIn is now used by recruiters and professionals far and wide. Ensure you have a profile that is up to date and is reflective of your experience and achievements.

  ii. Obtain online recommendations from clients, former colleagues, managers, etc. These will act as excellent informal references for you and you have control over what appears.

  iii. Online communities exist on LinkedIn and other sites where you can network with industry peers and those in similar occupations to share information and find out about new vacancies, as some employers also use these to post roles.

iv. Exclusive networking sites such as those run by your professional institute, educational alumni or business memberships are also useful forums to join to network, share ideas and experiences with peers and hear about new openings.

v. Research the most appropriate job boards for your career. Monster and TotalJobs etc are good all-rounder's but there are many that are specific to different careers. Recruiters and companies regularly use these to hire talent.

vi. Corporate websites – decide which companies you'd like to work for and target them directly.

vii. Companies often have a recruitment function - familiarise yourself with the individual in that team who recruits roles in your area – this will help ensure you are at the forefront of their mind when new vacancies come up.

viii. Who's the decision maker? Contact them directly through researching the role and then using the internet to establish who it reports into.

5

ix. Use the internet to research not only the company, but also the people who will be interviewing you, their background, speaking appearances, press interviews, etc.

x. Also use it to research the company's competitors and the competitive/market landscape that they operate in so that you can appear knowledgeable about the company's business and their key challenges. Companies like nothing more than proactive candidates who can really demonstrate they have made an effort.

For further insights and proven methods that give you an unfair advantage in the current job market, visit www.beajobmagnet.co.uk

Don't's

- Lengthy CVs are a real no-no. There is much debate around the optimum length of a CV with some claiming that 2 sides is the maximum. Speaking from experience as a recruiter and an employer, I don't think you should worry if you exceed this marginally. The key objective is to focus on your most relevant experience and achievements. Keep the details concise and relevant and don't provide reams of information about a role you did 15 years ago.

- Many people have a tendency to outline their responsibilities in their roles rather than key achievements, which are actually the things that differentiate you.

- In a highly competitive market you need to make your CV easy to disseminate. Lengthy paragraphs in a CV make it difficult for hiring managers and recruiters to identify the areas that they're interested in, so the use of bullet points can really help here.

Successful Interviewing

Ensuring that you have a well developed understanding of how potential employers interview is a critical step to securing employment. The number of times I have seen 'the perfect candidate' on paper not perform to their potential at interview is too frequent and disappointing.

First impressions count - make sure you are dressed in an appropriate manner to represent the culture of the employer you are interviewing with. If the interview is on a Friday, ask if it is dress down day and ask what that means in the business so that you are fitting in straight away.

Gone are the days when all you should expect from an interview is a detailed biographical overview of your career to date. Employers are getting much more sophisticated with interviewing and competency (or behavioural) based interviews are now used with regularity during the hiring process. Competency based interviewing is behavioural based lines of questioning grounded on the concept that past behaviour is a good barometer of future performance in a similar situation. It focuses on experiences, behaviours, knowledge, skills and abilities that are specifically job related.

5

Traditional interviews might have consisted of questions such as "Tell me about yourself." In contrast the process of competency based interviewing is much more probing and works very differently. Employers predetermine which specific skills are necessary for the job for which you are being interviewed, and then ask very direct questions to establish if you possess those skills.

For example, if a strong customer focus is necessary for a position, you may be asked to discuss a specific example in which you demonstrated exceptional customer focus, and they will then drill down further into your responses, probing more deeply as they go. A good way to work out which skills you may be assessed on, is to spend time reviewing the job description for the role, to pick out the core skills required. During a competency based interview, always listen carefully to the question, ask for clarification if necessary, and make sure you answer the question completely.

As part of your interview preparation, you should spend time identifying examples of situations from your career where you have demonstrated the behaviours required for the role. Remember that your responses need to be specific and detailed, not general, and make sure that you refresh your memory regarding your achievements in the past couple of years. Competency based questions can be challenging if you are not prepared, so also consider what the recruiter is trying to find out about you by asking you a particular question.

Examples of Competency Based Questions
- Demonstrate how you were able to influence someone to achieve a key business objective

- Give an example when you had to think on your feet to manage a challenging situation

- Identify a time in any particular role in which you were faced with problems or stresses that tested your skills

- Give an example of how you had to use your written communication skills in order to get an important point across

- Give me an example of an important goal that you had previously identified, and tell me about your success on achieving it

- Recall an event when you had to exceed your jobs responsibilities to achieve a business goal

A great tool for giving you the appropriate structure for this style of interview is the widely used **STAR method -Situation, Task, Action, Result.**

These steps enable you to briefly give an interviewer an overview of a situation, what you did specifically, and the positive result or outcome. This structure, combined with the 'toolkit' of examples that you have prepared before the interview will give you the best chance of success. The STAR method is outlined in greater detail below:

Situation: Describe a situation you were involved in that resulted in a positive outcome.

Task: Highlight the tasks that were involved in the situation.

Action: Discuss the variety of actions utilised in the situation's task.

Results: What results directly followed because of your actions.

Whenever you can, quantify your results. Numbers can serve to illustrate your degree of success or level of authority and responsibility very effectively. Also be prepared to provide examples of when results didn't turn out as you planned. What did you do then? What did you learn? Your potential employer will want to see how you react in the face of adversity.

For further insights and proven methods that give you an unfair advantage in the current job market, visit www.beajobmagnet.co.uk

ACTION  **POINTS**

If we look at this area of competency based interviewing, which ones of those questions could you comfortably answer and which ones couldn't you actually answer? Write it down!

_____

_____

_____

_____

_____

The ones you could answer – great, get them prepared because they are not going to change. There are only about 20 actual core competency questions that an organisation can humanly look at. If you are serious about focusing on being great at interviewing then you can you build your repertoire of responses as there is only a certain amount they can ever actually ask you.

As I have mentioned interviewing is still the single most successful way of actually getting an ideal career move. I am fascinated as to why certain individuals get a job and others do not. Certainly you need to have a certain level of qualification for a role but quite often a lot of it comes down to the attitude and the mindset of a candidate.

I have had some real howlers where candidates have been met at reception by the recruiter and whilst having a chat they asked if they managed to park easily. The candidate then replies that the parking was a bit of a nightmare. The whole interview then starts off on a negative footing. Even if this has been the case, the best reply would be to say "Oh it was fine, haven't you got lovely offices etc", build rapport, start it well.

Job Interview do's and don'ts

Do's

- **Know the company, its products and/or its service.** Have you used their product or know someone who has? Know the person you are meeting in every detail. Have they given speeches or written articles recently? What do they believe the industry trends are? They are likely to be on LinkedIn - so find them. Identify what their key business challenges are.

- **Rehearse your answers to the likely key questions you will be asked.** Visualise the interview being a success and how you will respond well in advance of the interview.

- **Find out what their 'pain points'** are in the business and demonstrate how you will solve them. This will be your first business action plan that you are presenting to them. If you are struggling to gain this information the top business considerations for any organisation are often linked to gaining new customers or up/cross selling, cutting costs and increasing loyalty of existing customers - these are the key growth drivers for any business.

- **Use the extensive research** you have conducted to confidently answer your questions accurately and precisely, don't be scared of a short break and a couple of seconds of silence; the interviewer may well be just thinking.

5

- **Ask appropriate questions.** One of the most effective questions to ask a line manager is what success will look like and how this role will be judged in the next 6 months. What that really does for you is it tells you exactly where their priorities are. You can tailor your communication to answer these questions, and by doing so you can then demonstrate how you will be part of that success. Identify what the vision is for the business, what challenges are they facing and how these challenges are being met.

- **Ask what steps** the organisation has taken to embrace social media and the opportunities presented by the internet.

- **Concluding the interview.** Ask the interviewers thoughts and if any point requires further clarification and finally what the next stage of the recruitment process will be.

- **Write a short thank you** note on e-mail with the purpose of maintaining dialogue regardless of the outcome of the interview.

Don'ts

- **Turn up late.** This will first and foremost mean that you have less time for the interview and you'll have to work extra hard to overcome the initial bad impression. If you are going to be late due to truly exceptional circumstances, make sure you call ahead.

- **Not being prepared.** All this demonstrates is that you are lazy, unprofessional and lacking interest in both the role and company – would you offer a job to someone like this?

- **Stumble over questions.** If you feel nervous, remember to take deep breaths; this will help you to relax and be able to think more clearly. You can also prepare and practice your answers to typical interview questions beforehand so that you are ready with the required information and are able to present it confidently to the interviewer.

- **Talk too much** - this is often a sign of nerves. Preparation and practice can help improve confidence and reduce nerves. Make sure you listen carefully to the question, and that your answers are relevant and focused. If you're not sure that you fully understand what is being asked of you, seek clarity from the interviewer. Always ask for a drink of water even if you don't want one; it gives a natural break for thinking through a difficult question without "umming" and "arring" etc.

- **Be Negative.** An interviewer will be looking to employ individuals with a positive attitude. Avoid speaking negatively about your previous employers, managers etc, and instead concentrate on the positives and your achievements.

- **Not having questions to ask.** Ensure you have some questions you want to ask your interviewer about the role, organisation, culture, business challenges etc. A healthy curiosity is a positive and shows you are truly interested in the opportunity.

5

In conclusion there is no substitute for preparation. Research the company, the interviewers and the role in depth (using your network, the internet, press). Along with preparing your 'toolkit' of real life examples you will be well on the road to interview success. Good luck!!

Going the extra mile and, despite lack of experience, still get the job

I had a fascinating situation recently where a candidate's attitude set him apart from all other candidates. I was recruiting a role for a rapidly growing mobile technology company who wanted an experienced person to add immediate value to their business. One particular candidate only had 18 months' actual experience, but the client was willing to look at him for what was a potentially far more senior role.

I secured them an interview and made the suggestion that they go into one of the stores and try out the new product so that they could get a feel for it. Responding, they explained that they wouldn't just go into the store to look at the product; they were actually going to purchase it. They wanted to use the handset and truly examine the customer experience. They would then develop a plan to demonstrate how they would improve the product. I thought, "Wow, this is a person who wants to get that job."

After a series of interviews they did get the role. At a later date I asked the line manager why they had chosen that particular candidate and they explained that their 'proactivity' had been the deciding factor. They proved that they could fit into their culture without ever being asked the question how do you demonstrate your initiative?

Where could you go the extra mile before your next interview?

One of my clients had asked me to source candidates for a Senior Communications role. When asking for feedback following the first stage of interviews they explained that one of my candidates stood head and shoulders above the others. This candidate was highly motivated and had carried out extensive research into their brand. They had visited a number of the company's stores and interviewed a variety of store managers to gain deeper insights into the business at customer interface level. At further interviews they utilised these insights to demonstrate how they would add value to the business. This candidate was offered the role and continues to have a significant impact on the growth of the brand.

5

Effective Presentation

All candidates need to present. Even if the interviewer asks you to tell them about yourself, this is a presentation. Make sure you practice so that you can confidently summarise who you are, how you are positioned and where you can add value. I still find many candidates not able to present themselves sufficiently effectively and make an appropriate impact.

Making effective and compelling presentations is increasingly being used by employers towards the latter part of a hiring process. It is clearly an opportunity to demonstrate your ideas, rigour of argument and your communication and influencing skills. Based on extensive personal and professional experience I would suggest investing extensively in training and finely tuning your ability in this career accelerating skill.

Learn from a master - Steve Jobs

Steve Jobs, co-founder and co-creator of Apple, was widely regarded as one of the best communicator in business. He used the Macworld events to spread the word to excite the Apple customers/ 'raving fans' on the latest Apple product launches (Gallo 2010).

So how did he achieve such excitement, interest and marketing success?

1. A very strong start to provoke curiosity with his audience.
2. He used images and music to bring the product demonstrations to life.
3. He told stories that took his audience on an engaging, fun and inspirational journey.
4. He used a 'WOW' moment to leave a lasting positive impression on his audience.

Do's

- Answer the question set by the panel.

- Set out the purpose of the presentation and the agenda so the audience is clear about the content.

- It is natural to feel nervous - the good news is that this means that the presentation matters to you. Use this to your advantage, have a positive strong start and the rest will flow.

- Engage all of the audience ensuring you capture their attention. Remember if they are in the room they are part of the decision making process.

- Engage each individual on the interview panel recognising their different business needs as early as possible within the presentation. Give a taste of why your presentation is important, what it will cover, how you will achieve results and allow questions to be asked.

- Be positive, friendly, and make and maintain regular eye contact.

- Keep still so the audience can focus on your message not potential distracting movements.

- Be appropriately dressed and well groomed; this will give you a huge confidence boost.

- Watch the reaction of your audience and adjust your energy and pace to keep them engaged and focused on you and your message. Pause, breathe and look for the reaction of the listener before moving onto the next point.

5

- Less is more. Use visual images and keep points short. If the presentation is 10 minutes with 5 minutes for questions, don't attempt to have 8 slides with 30 bullet points on each. I often see people cramming as much as possible on a slide thinking bigger is best - not so in this instance.

- Give your handouts at the end - you want peoples' attention during the presentation.

- Practice, practice, practice - the more deliberately you practice presenting, the better you will get at it.

- Anticipate likely questions that will be asked and have prepared answers.

- Clearly demonstrate your passion for the subject by communicating with enthusiasm.

- Use your experience of the subject and make the presentation your own; bring out your own personality when you are selling your position.

- Present your case persuasively by tuning into the values of the audience.

- Remember the presentation is about what you can do for that potential company and what your achievements are. Think of the benefits of what you can bring to the party.

For further insights and proven methods that give you an unfair advantage in the current job market, visit www.beajobmagnet.co.uk

Dont's

- Be unprepared and try to wing it!

- Waffle or become distracted by a seemingly uninterested audience member.

- Get on your high horse about your pet parts of the presentation - stay fully focused.

- Have a low level of energy; your body language will speak far louder than your words.

- Make 10 points+ on a single slide.

- Focus on style over substance – combine a balance of both.

- Get defensive when asked challenging questions – this is part of the process.

- Read the slides – your attention and focus should be your audience.

- Fail to back up your answers with results and achievements.

5

ACTION  POINTS

1. Always have an up to date CV, whether you are actively looking for a new role or not. Every three months write down your achievements; this will remind you of your successes and also keep you up to date to take advantage of any opportunity presented to you. What have been your greatest quantifiable achievements in the last 2 years of your career?

5

2. Prepare yourself for your next interview like never before. Whether you are passively looking or actively looking, there are always going to be opportunities to present yourself. An interviewer is likely to focus on your achievements within the areas of influence, leadership, communication, change and flexibility; know how to demonstrate them in a compelling way. Preparation is the key to success. What examples do you have that would be a compelling way of demonstrating your key skills?

5

3. When attending interviews know the background of the interviewers via their LinkedIn profile and consider how you will match your pitch to their needs. Which high profile industry figures could you research on LinkedIn?

5

4. Be an effective presenter. There is no quicker way to elevate yourself as a brand than being able to speak in front of a group of influential people; you will be viewed as an expert. The highest paid people in business are typically not paid just because of their functional experience. Most are rewarded because they are able to communicate, motivate and inspire others to actions. Take every opportunity to present in any environment - it will build your confidence.

What opportunities could you create to practise and enhance this critical skill in your career armoury?

5

5

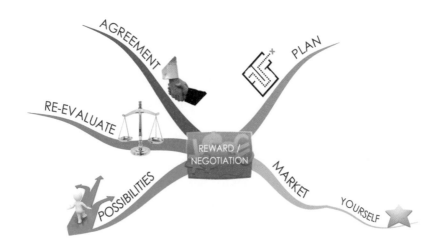

Secret 6

Effective Negotiation - the missing link that ensures you are being appropriately rewarded for the value you add

I urge you to consider how you can ensure that you always make the right career move and have a rethink about the value you add to a business.

You are a unique individual and you bring your own distinctive experience, value and perspective to the field of expertise you are in. People who are highly paid in any industry have earned that right because they take on more responsibility, duties and added value. They have also learnt to influence and 'position' themselves effectively.

In my experience many people don't realise the value they add to an organisation. When it comes to your career move, always remember you have done a huge amount of work to even get to offer stage; you have earned the right to be appropriately rewarded for that particular job.

Having used the key tools throughout this book to position yourself as an employee of high potential the final stage of agreeing terms with your new employer is vital. You have gone through some rigorous interview stages; you have come to the conclusion that this is the best company for you and one where you are going to be spending a substantial amount of time over the next few years. This is a considerable investment for you so making and taking the time to calmly and confidently plan your negotiation effectively is absolutely critical.

The good news is the further you move up the ladder of an organisation, the greater access you have to key decision makers resulting in a greater opportunity to influence. This allows you to negotiate your salary/package and benefits on a one to one basis rather than the systematic negotiation undertaken further down the organisation.

Set yourself up for success from day 1

When you start in your new position you want to be confident from day one that you haven't sold yourself short and that your new employer has got a bit of a bargain when they recruited you. You are probably going to spend at least two to three years in the organisation; you might well spend more. Knowing in your mind that you have everything lined up where possible for you to be successful is absolutely critical. I have seen people go into roles where they have undersold themselves and this has caused misalignment and even resentment further down the line.

Ideally you want to continue to be motivated and also you want to send a signal to your future employer that this is a peer relationship, it is a win-win scenario for both of you. To set yourself up for success it is best to get the relationship off on an equal footing. Negotiation is an interactive process of give and take and the overriding objective must be to always keep lines of communication open and to avoid aggressive or threatening tactics. Stay in rapport with the people you are actually doing business with, always keep the conversations appropriate, friendly, professional and with a win-win outcome in mind.

A key element to realise when using this model is to appreciate that any negotiation is a fine balancing act. If you have a skill set and mindset that is in high demand and you find yourself in a place where you have 3 or 4 offers, you can obviously play a smart game that is highly lucrative for yourself whilst still maintaining the relationships. If you find you only have one offer and you know that the culture of the organisation you are joining would not appreciate a negotiated approach then be mindful of this when trying to secure the final contract and be careful in your messaging and communication.

6

The SMART system - A proven 5 step framework for making the right decisions in your career and being appropriately rewarded

Start from a well defined plan

Market yourself as a premium employee

A range of possible solutions and options

Re-evaluate all information

Together have you reached an agreement that works for both parties?

Step 1: Start from a well defined plan

i. Remind yourself why you are actively looking to leave your present company and how these frustrations will be solved by taking a career move. How does this career move enhance your movement towards your long term career goals?

ii. Using the table overleaf, write down the 12 most important criteria of a career move for yourself and score them out of 10; this brings a considered approach to your decision. When you total up these scores you need to be looking for a score in excess of 90 for an ideal career move. You can gain a view on the bigger picture by comparing the value of each career option. The overriding element in evaluation is to look at the gut/intuition score, this is a critical factor. If you have high scores for a career overall but a low score on what your intuition is telling you it may be time to re-evaluate. In my experience the following criteria provide the foundation when evaluating the right career move:

Criteria	Career Option 1	Career Option 2	Career Option 3
Industry Sector Growth potential			
The Company - its employer brand and reputation			
The challenges & Autonomy of the Role			
Ability of the line manager to realise your potential			
Career Prospects			
Base salary			
Car allowance			
Bonus Potential			

6

Criteria	Career Option 1	Career Option 2	Career Option 3
How this role fits into your long term career goal and plan			
Location			
Training and personal development potential			
Your Intuition/Gut feeling			
TOTAL			

6

iii. Conduct research on how other similar and comparable roles are paid and the associated benefits in your industry.

iv. Write down what your key message and theme are. This will form the agenda to be used during the negotiation process, they will act as your guidepost at all times and clarifies your message and intentions.

v. Plan for how you will respond when some of your requests are declined. Commit to staying in rapport and have a platform of open dialogue despite any difficulties or challenges during the process, take none of the tactics used as a personal affront on you.

Step 2: Market yourself as a premium employee

i. Clearly understand the responsibilities/duties and key performance indicator's and how you will be judged in this role – this identifies the value you will add to an organisation. Remember during the course of this recruitment process you will have positioned yourself as the ideal choice for this role at this particular time.

ii. Clearly understand the interests and desires of your potential employer by asking them to identify what their business goals are when making this appointment and what problems it will solve or opportunities it will create.

6

iii. Identify the upper and lower limits of the benefit package you are prepared to accept. Split this into must have, nice to have and possibilities but not essentials.

Step 3: A range of possible solutions and options

i. Know what your future employer can be flexible on and what they cannot; remember you may be joining an organisation with established salary bands and most companies are very keen to stick to established norms in terms of base salary and benefits package. Early reviews, promotion for exceptional performance, are potential areas to explore as a route to increasing your value. Seek and qualify what the common ground is, this is where agreement will be struck.

This due diligence will allow you to confidently answer the question what salary package and benefits you desire.

ii. Start the process by making respectful requests and tentative agreements. As an example if you wish for an early review make this request and clearly demonstrate under what terms you are receiving this e.g. achievement of key performance indictors 10% ahead of target. There must be a clear business benefit communicated to the employer for a positive outcome.

iii. Watch for peoples' reactions and non-verbal responses rather than words, as these speak volumes in themselves. Try and remember not to take this situation and yourself too seriously; this is an important situation for your career but if you can create an environment of respect and harmony, all things remain possible.

iv. It is fundamental that you make your future employer aware of your salary expectations, before they make an offer – to achieve this have a consistent and appropriate message. This approach has consistently led to individuals

6

being rewarded at a higher rate. Your message could be, "Your company is my preferred career option because of the opportunities presented. I would like to ensure that I am appropriately rewarded due to the value I will add in shaping the operational efficiencies of the business over the next 6 months," or "How I will be shaping the key growth strategy/execution in a key market over the next 6 months?"

v. If some of your requests require authority from higher up the organisation, you ideally want to have a relationship with that person so you can influence and demonstrate your value. Be patient during this critical stage. Time delays are often due to the fact that this negotiation is not the only key business priority of that decision maker on that day. Remain clear on your objectives and allow the process to run its course. Agreeing to time scales after each action will allow the process to maintain momentum. Be flexible on how the process evolves - you might even be positively surprised.

I had a situation recently where a decision maker took longer over making an offer than initially expected. However, rather than coming back with an attractive bonus of 40%, they came back with 50%; this forward thinking client clearly understood how to motivate future employees to ensure a win-win situation.

For further insights and proven methods that give you an unfair advantage in the current job market, visit www.beajobmagnet.co.uk

Step 4: Re-evaluate all information

i. If you know this is not an opportunity you are likely to consider, I urge you to inform all parties and stakeholders as soon as possible; this will help to maintain all relationships. There is nothing more frustrating for employers when they have spent significant time creating an offer, to be told 24 hours later that the candidate is withdrawing after having a surprise idea come out of nowhere!

ii. When you receive the offer from the company, go back to your established criteria for choosing the best career move for yourself. Use the table overleaf as analysis to measure all aspects of the benefits package you are currently receiving and those of your career options. Writing all the information down brings an objective approach and will allow you to compare your current terms with those offered by your offers.

6

Criteria	Career Option 1	Career Option 2
Basic Salary		
Bonus		
Other Incentives		
Pension		
Private Medical Insurance		
Life Assurance		
Permanent Health Insurance		
Travel Insurance		
Gym/Club Membership		
Training		
TOTAL		

6

iii. The relationship with your future employer is the most valuable aspect in this process. Remember, how you negotiate will be perceived as a direct reflection on how you are likely to conduct yourself for the company after joining them. Always remember, win-win and make requests from decision makers that they can deliver on and not for things that could potentially make them lose face.

iv. Keep notes and all communication in writing. Always sleep on any offer overnight.

Step 5: Together have you reached an agreement that works for both parties?

i. When you have reached a verbal agreement and you are committed to joining an organisation, withdraw from any other recruitment processes, thanking the other party for their time and flexibility.

ii. If you have not been able to reach agreement, take the time to explain to the company why your decision not to join them has been made. Both the organisation and yourself will have invested significant time and resources to get this far. Continue to invest in the relationship; remember this is an organisation you were seriously considering joining.

iii. Ensure that any verbal agreements have been included in the written contract that you sign. If there are aspects that you do not understand or require further clarification on, seek specialist advice from an employment lawyer rather than a generalist.

6

iv. When you are happy that the contract is a written representation of what you agreed verbally, sign the contract and return as soon as possible.

v. Plan your resignation and how you can exit your present organisation in a professional manner to maintain your reputation. Although this is not always possible, remember that the business world is a small place and you will certainly cross paths with your current peer group and line manager in the future.

An example of a professionally managed win-win agreement

I recently worked with a candidate and by using the above formula we were able to secure an ideal career move and raise their overall salary and package by 48%. We were able to achieve this because they clearly understood their motivations for moving and had established the criteria they would use to evaluate any new options. The candidate was fully aware of the value they would add to the new organisation and how they would be judged in terms of key operational efficiencies. They had set clear agendas for meetings and a theme based around a win-win outcome maintaining a professional manner throughout. Their due diligence throughout the process ensured that on day one they had secured an excellent career move and set themselves and their new employer up for success from day one.

For further insights and proven methods that give you an unfair advantage in the current job market, visit www.beajobmagnet.co.uk

6

How not to negotiate towards your desired outcome

A number of years ago I was working with a candidate who wanted to work for a highly sought after employer. The organisation in question had an exceptional leadership team, market leading products and provided exceptional career prospects. I was able to find a suitable role with significant career stretch for this candidate; they felt that the role and company were an ideal fit for their career development and long term goals.

I secured them a generous salary package increase. They were very pleased with the offer but they wondered if the company would offer a little more. We both knew that this employer had already stretched the salary/package boundaries quite significantly and this request was probably over the edge. I urged the candidate to look at the whole picture and to see that this was a very attractive offer and was beyond the highest level of expectation they had anticipated when starting the recruitment process.

6

Despite this advice, the candidate insisted that they were worth more; I advised them that the client may well push back and as a result of us pushing so hard may well withdraw the offer. The candidate insisted that we try. It led to the CEO pulling the job offer and not wanting to speak to the candidate again. This was disappointing on many fronts as not only was the candidate not able to take up an ideal career but the trust and relationship with the potential employer was so damaged that no future communication was possible for them.

Striking the right balance and understanding the needs and desires of future employers is a vital component to successful win-win negotiation agreements. Knowing how to negotiate and when to stop is a key to success.

Do and don'ts for successful win-win negotiation

Do's

- Be very clear on what your outcomes and goals are. It is critical that you identify what organisation you want to join, the type of culture you want to be part of, the products/services you want to work with and the salary you expect.

- You need to get into the mindset of the decision maker. This is where negotiation gets interesting - what do they want most? When you actually understand that, you can start to realise how valuable you will be to them.

- Value the relationship with the decision maker and others involved in the process. Despite any challenges, commit to remaining calm and focussed on the end result.

6

- Do know what your upper and lower limits of all factors are.

- Do maintain rapport and responsiveness at all points.

- Do seek a win-win outcome – this is an extended interview so how you act now will be critical to how you conduct yourself moving forward.

- Be absolutely clear as to what the employers' current situation is. Always focus on the relationship, the agenda and what your core message is.

Deliberate and specific preparation will allow you to achieve greater financially reward.

Don'ts

- Be unprepared and having not considered the other side's perspective.

- Be too demanding thus failing to stay in rapport and respecting the employer's points of view.

- Make requests that the individual has no authority to deliver.

- Hold an unrealistic value of yourself, failing to recognise your future employer's constraints.

- Mismanage your own reputation during these times as you never know when you will encounter the person again. Always leave the door open and keep the theme and tone professional, friendly and engaging.

6

- Focus on just the salary; consider the whole picture of career opportunities, personal development, bonus, mentoring and growth opportunities.

Recently I secured an offer for a candidate who stated that everything about the opportunity was perfect; the role, the organisation, and the chance to learn and be mentored, thus expanding their skill set. They wanted a 25% increase in salary; I was able to secure them 22%. They declined the opportunity being completely focused on securing 25%. Needless to say they have stayed at their existing organisation and carried on earning 22% less than they could have achieved in their ideal career.

6

ACTION POINTS

1. Learn how to negotiate more effectively. Start valuing yourself as a unique individual and as a person of value. What areas of your negotiation structure technique do you believe you could improve on?

_____

_____

_____

_____

_____

2. Start win/win negotiating in all aspects of your life and believe you are going to get better at it. Start negotiation on small things that don't matter too much. Have a script for any negotiation; preparation means that you are more likely to achieve your outcome. What are the objectives from your next salary review and how are you going to achieve them using the SMART method?

_____

_____

_____

_____

_____

6

3. Write down the 12 most important parts of a career move for you.

_____

_____

_____

_____

_____

_____

_____

4. Have a detailed plan ready before you start actively looking for career opportunities of how you will choose and evaluate your next career move.

_____

_____

_____

_____

_____

6

6

What employers **really** desire

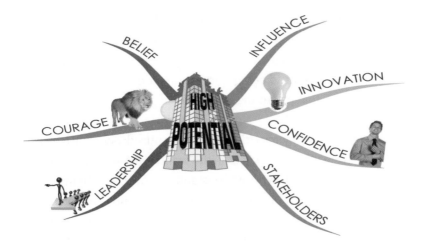

Secret 7

Discover the elusive secrets of being a person of high potential.

Having been responsible for many senior appointments, I fully understand how recruitment decisions are made and how the CEO and board identify and distinguish the skills of high potential employees from those of good functional employees. My goal in this chapter is to introduce the skills that are most valued and how you can systematically master each one of them to give you even greater career choice.

7

How is it that certain people seem to have the careers of their choice and accelerate their progress regardless of economic situation? What takes them from being good managers, good functional specialists to being leaders, directors and CEOs. What is the difference that makes the difference?

Breakthrough commercial ideas are highly prized; one only has to think of the leading companies in the world like Amazon, Apple, Google and Facebook who are constantly re-inventing themselves. Imagine if you were able to have a flow of ideas and systems that lead to you being seen as an innovation leader. Rapid change is the constant, with effective influence, the ability to lead, inspire trust and action in others as the key skills of our time.

Mastery of these skills ensures that you will never be worried or fearful in your career and you will always be moving in the right direction - upwards. It is fundamental to note that developing each of these skills takes time and focused practice and execution; I would recommend choosing one at a time to focus on, develop and ultimately master.

7

Influence

Why is the skill of influence so well sought after?

Influence can be viewed as having the ear of decision makers. This ensures your message has a soft landing and has the appropriate platform to be listened to, evaluated and potentially added to the strategy of an organisation. Without this route of influence, your ideas do not have the platform to fly or you the opportunity to shine.

What is influence?

Mastery of influence is the ability to understand the organisational culture, its key drivers and the core motivations of the fundamental decisions makers. Key influencers are able to energise their ideas by building a consensus of collaborative mindshare. They can overcome objections which allow these ideas to be implemented for commercial success. The very best influencers are able to lead and pass on this skill.

A compelling example of positive influence occurred during 2006 when Bill Gates was able to influence Warren Buffett to donate $37 billion of his own money to the Bill and Melinda Gates foundation. This is considered to be the largest ever donation by one individual in the history of the human race (BBC news 2006). This donation led to the Bill and Melinda Gates foundation having greater resources than the United Nations.

This is a relationship that has evolved over many years built on a strong bond of mutual liking, trust and respect between both Gates and Buffett.

Despite wanting to share his wealth, Buffett had been reluctant to donate to charities in the past, as he was concerned that they were

7

not equipped to continue to create wealth and multiply the effects of the money to help others. Gates has an incredible track record of creating wealth and is now using this to eradicate the top 20 diseases in the world. The critical element that achieved this outcome was that Gates had Buffett's ear and used this to influence him to share resources for the common good.

How to increase your sphere of influence

The framework presented here has been developed by Dr Robert Cialdini, who is considered to be the leading authority on the subject and has tested and proven 'the weapons of influence' (2007).

The 6 weapons are:

1. The Law of reciprocity/reciprocation (give and take)
2. Social proof (does that person comply to the value set of other people?)
3. Authority
4. Commitment and consistency (accepted rules)
5. Liking or being like somebody.
6. Scarcity (the rule of few)

After extensive study and research, Cialdini concludes that these 6 weapons can be used to effectively influence any situation where there is human interaction.

This was clearly demonstrated in an extensive study conducted at Citibank across various international locations (Goldstein.N, et al. 2007). Citibank employees were asked to identify what would motivate them to feel most obligated to help colleagues with a major project that pulled them away from their own work.

7

- UK, Canada and USA responded by asking themselves what that person had done for them recently? (Reciprocity)
- Germany and Scandinavian regions response was to identify what the rules and regulations within the organisation were to deal with such a request. (Commitment and consistency)
- Far Eastern response questioned how this person was associated to a higher authority within the organisation. (Authority)
- Spain responded by asking how that person was connected to my friends. (Liking)

Within the same organisation, the answers varied significantly, but we can see that the answers followed Cialdini's laws. So how can you use these insights to develop greater influence?

People have critical conversations every day that have a significant influence on the relationships they ultimately build within organisations. Effective planning of your meetings, e-mails and calls will ensure that you can begin to create the outcomes you require. By understanding what your relationship is with the individual, what their needs are and how you should tailor your communication will lead to a greater probability of success.

In my experience, the law of reciprocity is the single most powerful one to be used when conducting business in the UK and USA. Having studied exceptionally successful people, most if not all are givers. A key mentor of mine, Ross Wilson, is a highly sought after business strategy advisor and never short of business and opportunities. He is always giving time and advice to people and with no expectation of immediate return - good things always come back to him.

7

Social Proof

When you are looking for a recommendation of a new supplier for your business or for a major individual purchase, people first ask within their peer group and network for recommendations. Most people interpret this as acting in accordance with what is the social norm. You can use this in business by focusing on the trendsetters within groups as they set out what is the social norm behaviour. Leading consumer brands do this regularly, commonly referring to it as a seeding strategy.

Authority

People obey experts and authority so crafting yourself a niche as a guru or an expert in your field will build your brand and increases your influence.

Commitment and consistency

Writing a goal down and publically sharing it demonstrates commitment and a likely consistency of action, a powerful source of influence.

Liking or being like somebody

Ultimately people are easily persuaded by people they like and people who are like them. Building rapport and trust with those you want to influence is the first step to evolving a long term relationship.

Scarcity

I believe that Richard Branson uses this to great effect when trying to fund new projects. People want to be part of any deal associated with him because there is only one Richard Branson and that great business idea could go elsewhere and that opportunity missed.

Being aware that a toolkit exists to influence any situation in a moment or to build engaged consensus over time is very useful, however, the real skill is in the application of these tools and using them when most appropriate to enhance your influence on any outcome.

For further insights and proven methods that give you an unfair advantage in the current job market, visit www.beajobmagnet.co.uk

7

Innovation

Why is innovation so highly sought after?

We live in a dynamical changing world where the pace of change is increasing on a daily basis. Seemingly impossible tasks and breakthroughs are occurring on a daily basis, the internet and its components of social networking are changing the very face of how we work, live and play.

Most successful businesses are innovation led companies, with some focusing on minor refinements and others on bold new steps. Every business needs innovation to move forward, and all of these companies require innovation leaders. Recently we have seen the emergence of previously unheard of job titles like Chief Innovation Officer and VP of Innovation.

What is being innovative?

Mastery of innovation comes from an insatiable curiosity of how new possibilities can be purposefully applied and consistently systemised to solve business problems.

During the last 20 years, a number of people stand out as real innovators; Bill Gates (Former CEO of Microsoft), Mark Zuckerberg (CEO of Facebook), Evan Williams (co-founder of Twitter), all of whom have created significant platforms that have transformed our lives on a daily basis.

The stand out person for me as the game changing catalyst has to be the inventor of the World Wide Web - Tim Berners-Lee, (Johnson 2010). Every aspect of our modern life has been transformed by the World Wide Web. This was a side project Berners-Lee was developing whilst working at CERN (European Organisation for

Nuclear Research) and started as a way to organise his own data, then other people's data and after many versions the full vision of the World Wide Web was born. For the continued advancement of business opportunities and for the human race the world needs leaders like Tim Berners-Lee to see and create new possibilities.

How to be an innovative leader

We live in a world of ambiguity and I know one of the key challenges for many people not embracing change and being catalysts for its development is the fear of what those changes could mean for them. As human beings we are built for change and when we are asked or sometimes forced to up our game we typically are able to respond by challenging previously accepted norms of beliefs and performance. I know that top achievers who excel at getting ahead in their careers master this skill. They either learn to become adaptable and flexible, or they are the leaders who are in control of the situation and as such leading the change.

In the technology industry, ambiguity is the norm and changes occur at an alarming rate. Products are launched consistently and there is no certainty if a product is going to be commercially successful. The technological explosion maintains momentum; you can connect with anybody in the world and have your own TV channel for less than £200 by buying a flip camera and utilising YouTube. Change presents possibilities but it can still be a daunting prospect.

The key to embracing change is to plan and have your own vision of your future. Ask yourself what does this change potentially mean to my career? Clarity of what you want to achieve will enable you to move forward and act as a change agent within the organisation. Alternatively you may determine that alternative environments may well present better career opportunities. From an employer's

7

mindset, people resistant to change quickly get labelled and don't become involved in the key strategic projects. Being able to develop and complete change projects will allow you to demonstrate high value in an organisation as it evolves and develops.

When I met the innovation director of a Global premium brand we discussed his task of consistently delivering breakthrough commercial successes. We were reflecting on why his last innovation had been one of the most successful in consumer marketing and I asked him how he developed an innovation system. He explained that they needed to think and do things differently from the previous product. They had to challenge current thinking and utilise customer insights and trends. However the real skill came in the ability to anticipate the next trends and sometimes you have to take a quantum leap.

Learn from a master - Steve Jobs

Steve Jobs had a phenomenal team around him and Apple produce great products. He created an environment where product design and function was highly prized and where excellence was the norm. This was often down to a superior customer experience and technological innovation.

Jobs relentlessly explored ideas from many fields and in particular the liberal arts. His well documented passion for calligraphy led to the first set of beautifully designed products in the technology industry. This is the reason why every computer worldwide has different fonts to choose from. His real skill was joining the dots of possibilities and creating an innovation environment based on excellence, which repeatedly created success and added value to customers and shareholders alike.

The driving force behind the Apple innovation process is the brilliant British designer Sir Jonathan Ive who has a very resourceful attitude to innovation. He approaches design by trying to achieve the very most with the very least, resulting in maintaining simplicity (Gallo 2011).

In my experience Incremental steps of change and innovation are achieved with the questions How, What, When and Whom? The starting point of any great breakthroughs occurs in every field when the challenging and abstract questions are asked such as "What if?" or "Why not?"

Ask yourself if you could explore outside your comfort zone for ideas, inspiration and innovation? How could you create systems to bring these ideas to practical application? Think about industry blogs, customer forums, look outside your existing sphere of ideas i.e. what are the young generation interested in exploring?

7

Assured confidence

Why is assured confidence so highly sought?

Individuals both in organisations and society as a whole are looking for direction and confident leaders who display an assuredness and a certainty that people will follow. This was highlighted during the last recession which saw many struggling both mentally and emotionally to see beyond the current situation to the bigger picture where opportunities still existed. The confident leaders displayed a belief in their own and their organisation's ability to use challenging times as the springboard to even greater success.

Andy Street, Managing Director of John Lewis, is an example of a confident and considered leader. Even during the most challenging of times he continued to stay committed to the John Lewis approach of exceptional customer service. The partnership model where customers are served by the owners of the business appears to allow them to outstrip the performance of many of their competitors.

What is assured confidence?

Mastery of this skill is demonstrated by being bold enough to pursue a route and goal that is seemingly impossible combined with the balance of exercising sound judgement. This leads to confident leaders making consistently appropriate decisions whilst taking advantage of market opportunities. Confident people focus on training themselves to act in an appropriate, calm and controlled way in any given situation. They trust that they will make the best decision possible with the resources they have, accepting the results and feedback they receive.

7

How to build assured confidence – a daily discipline

Roger Bannister had an assured belief that a human being was able to run a sub four minute mile. After he had achieved this breakthrough many more people quickly achieved this previously impossible milestone. Bannister's attitude and mindset to this challenge was demonstrated clearly when he stated that, "however ordinary each of us may seem, we are all in some way special and can do things that are extraordinary, perhaps until then even thought impossible." (2004).

Self confidence and self belief is built over time and is a function of the results you have achieved. Your emotional state is critical to your level of confidence. In my experience the most successful people are able to see the opportunity presented in every challenging situation. By setting major career goals, challenges along the way are inevitable but can be confidently overcome.

Confidence is a moment to moment state of mind so you must constantly be aware of what you are thinking and how you are thinking it. Usually it is our own self talk where the demons start to create doubt in our mind; fear creeps in and takes away our confidence. If you look at the world around you and have the perspective that opportunities exist, you will find those opportunities; if you look for problems, that's what you will attract. I would encourage you to focus on overcoming your demons and limiting beliefs, by developing routines that ensure you always have access to your self confidence.

All great performers are nervous pre event; they have set routines for channelling their emotion to consistently produce the desired outcomes. Those who excel in their performance e.g. Olympic athletes, actors and successful business achievers, have all trained their mind to visualise being a success. They create positive images

7

in their mind of what they need to do. It is not that they are either confident or unconfident; critically it is how they are feeling in the moment and what resources they perceive they have access to. This creates their state of mind before they actually go into an event or meeting.

All behaviour is dependent on your state and obviously all your behaviour produces the results you have. If you can connect your mind to being in a positive, resourceful state where you have a positive physiology and psychology, you can have positive actions which will move you towards your goals more effectively. It doesn't mean everything is going to go your way, however you have given yourself the best possible opportunity to achieve.

Tools that will help develop your confidence

Expand your existing comfort zone step by step. The process of developing greater self confidence is achieved only when you actually do rather than think about doing. When you experience something new, irrespective of whether you succeed or fail, you will grow from the experience. The opportunity to learn from the experience will allow you to realise that you have achieved more than you previously thought. This is how we learn throughout life, as children this is how we learnt to walk.

Remind yourself of your career successes to date. Once a quarter, review your successful business contributions and write them down in a journal. This is effective for a number of reasons; firstly it charts your progress and makes you feel good and secondly you are reminding your brain of how successful you have been. It provides a permanent reference point to refer back to when new challenges occur.

It is also useful to identify feelings of confidence you have previously experienced and bring those feelings back to assist you in a challenging situation. Ask yourself what you saw when you felt confident, what did you hear, and what did you say to yourself? So that when you are feeling unconfident about a situation, you can remind yourself of the experiences you felt at a time when you were confident. These feelings will come back to you, you can then use these resources to maximise your chance of success in your new situation.

For further insights and proven methods that give you an unfair advantage in the current job market, visit www.beajobmagnet.co.uk

7

Does the CEO know about your results?

Why is this important?

To get ahead in your career, being able to prioritise your key actions and produce results quickly is a must have skill in the constantly changing business environment. If you don't have exposure to the board and the CEO does not know your results, your lack of visibility will harm your career progression. Having achieved positive results on a consistent basis, you must communicate them effectively.

What is being a recognised at board level ?

Mastery of the CEO knowing your results is not about being on social terms with the board (although it can help), or just communicating your team's results. This skill is about going above and beyond your daily responsibilities to anticipate and solve business problems that add significant sustainable value to the organisation. Naturally by consistently being a high performer in your day job, you earn the right to have a seat at the table to communicate with the board.

How to demonstrate your results to the board

Here is a clear demonstration of deliverable action that was noted and appreciated by the board of a major blue chip business. An individual had a deep rooted passion for exceptional customer service; although this was not part of his functional day job. He wanted to develop innovative systems that led to improved customer service and resulted in increased customer loyalty. The person in question developed a plan, interviewed customers, understood their frustrations and needs, and over time made the connections and systems to solve many of the existing problems.

Most importantly he connected with a key sponsor to ensure his ideas had a platform and were heard by the appropriate decision makers. Due to his initiative and effective communication skills, he is now viewed by the board as a person of exceptional future potential.

I would urge you to develop a stakeholder map of the key influencers in your business and what the impact of solving their primary business issues would have on your career. Keep a journal to plan, develop and chart your success; this process also builds your confidence and reminds you of your career direction and achievements.

7

The ultimate career accelerating skill

Why are effective leadership skills so important to become successful and well rewarded in your career?

Business organisations are interested in their success both now and in the future. The foundations of a company are supported by a structure of people. I know that the ability to engage people and lead them in empowering actions that achieve organisational goals is at the heart of that success.

It is clear that being a good leader and achieving results via others is a vital skill to have if you want to have a successful career in business. There are obviously people who are naturally talented leaders and there are people who are not natural leaders who still achieve excellent results via their people. Leadership is a set of decisions, behaviours and actions rather than just a personality trait. Many of the most effective leaders have proven methodology that they follow to achieve consistent results.

We have just been through a significant financial crisis and it became evident that in times of crisis people look for leadership. They seek hope and inspiration that despite the current difficulties they can weather the storm and still achieve.

I know that during challenging times you want to be supported by people who have faced difficulties previously and know how to make the right decisions. On thriving his third recession Ross Wilson (a key mentor of mine), explained what his thoughts and key strategies were on continued success. He firmly believed that challenging times are when you learn the most, because you are tested and your resources are stretched. He felt that his business would come out of this period in better shape because of the decisions made and skills gained.

What is leadership?

Leadership is the ability to set a direction for other people to follow you in. This allows people to go from where they are now to where you actually want them to be. Motivation comes from within these people, and as an effective leader you must create the environment to nurture their motivation and thus achieve the results. Typically, effective leaders have a high level of urgency, personal commitment and ambition for the business.
I recently asked the CEO of a leading mobile business, what the difference is between his individual contributors and leaders. He responded by explaining that leaders inspire action in others and create systems that make success a repeatable and scalable process again and again.

I know that good leaders don't just add and contribute; they multiply the effect of being in an organisation. Rather than being able to just add another block of revenue or another set of products they are able to effectively influence people around them and inspire action. Many of us have been fortunate to come across some great leaders at certain points in our career. Personally these leaders were able to inspire me; they were able to achieve their goals whilst making me feel good about achieving mine.

How do you develop great leadership traits and continue to grow as a leader?

Having the ambition to want to be a very good leader is a great start. Committing to learn from others and apply their strategies in appropriate situations will lead to improvement. It is worth identifying some leaders whom you admire, and ask them how they specifically lead and motivate their people. Attending events and speeches to note the methodology of successful leaders is a key way to learn.

7

Two leaders I resonance with are Tim Smit, CEO of The Eden Project, and Stuart Rose, former CEO of Marks and Spencer: Tim Smit for his ability to stretch and create a vision whilst maintaining his connection with all stakeholders, Stuart Rose for his skill as a communicator. He was interviewed at an IOD annual convention in what was a very challenging year for business; his message and grace of delivery was truly inspiring.

He explained that to be an effective leader you have got to be believable and realistic and still put a smile on people's faces. Employees need to come into work and believe there are going to be better days ahead. He is an optimist and he felt that having a deep rooted self-belief is extremely important to becoming a successful leader. Having a big vision is a key dimension but achieving it with small consistent daily steps shows believability. He believed that effective leaders keep an eye on the big picture whilst maintaining a focus on daily planning, and what they are going to achieve today.

How to demonstrate key leadership on a daily basis.

In addition to the key skills presented in this chapter thus far the following daily actions will enhance your effectiveness as a leader.

Walking the walk as well as talking the talk.

Being a role model and conducting yourself with integrity where your actions match your words is the most positive leadership trait I have experienced. A key client who I consider to be an 'employer of choice' does this consistently. Any candidate who meets her typically has a very positive experience and is keen to work for her - she is renowned for her actions rather than just her 'talk'.

I am sure we have all been in situations where a leader or line manager has a different set of standards for themselves, one rule for them and one rule for everyone else. Ask yourself were they able to effectively lead you?

What does that misalignment between actions and words lead to? An erosion of trust over a period of time.

Knowing what gets your people out of bed each day other than just money

Having a genuine interest in your team, their desires and goals for life will have a major impact on how you are perceived as a leader. People want to be heard, their ideas listened to and their views respected. As a leader you should seek to create the forum for open discussion, however decision making and results remain your ultimate responsibility.

7

Autonomy

I know most people go to work and use potentially less than a third of their talents. I am always amazed that when people are given a forum to express their ideas the creativity can really flow, and some excellent commercial opportunities can be created by people who may be perceived as quite far down the organisational chart. Allowing your team to express their talents can lead to a highly motivated and productive team. Google has committed to giving engineering employees 20% of their time to work on non-work related projects and then report back their results. This has led to some of the most successful commercial breakthroughs for the business such as Gmail and Google News.

Courage and belief

Believing in yourself and your ideas. This entails having well constructed arguments that back up your ideas that will stand up to scrutiny from a business perspective. I recall an interview with the managing director of a very successful software business who stated that people who come up with potential ideas really annoy him. I was shocked!

He explained that he valued employees who came to him with a winning business plan that would take the business forward. He suggested that they would have identified potential problems and by allowing others to challenge the idea develop multiple solutions which de-risked the business plan thus increasing the chance of success.

Open and responsive to feedback

Effective leaders are able to evolve and adapt over time to situations. They have the ability to inspire, engage and recruit great talent into their organisation. They use feedback to keep on raising the standards so that their people remain motivated and challenged within that business and ultimately these people in turn go on to be great leaders themselves.

Steve Jobs was reported to have had perfectionist tendencies coupled with an expectation of excellence. Potentially this could lead to a micro management style. However what is pretty obvious is that there are very talented people who bend over backwards to work for Apple and produce extraordinary results.

Effective leadership is not about results at any cost. It is how the results are achieved and how people are engaged that is highly prized because that is what can lead to repeatable and scalable success which is the very basis of any valuable business success.

For further insights and proven methods that give you an unfair advantage in the current job market, visit www.beajobmagnet.co.uk

ACTION POINTS

1. Identify how you can become a person of influence within your organisation and industry.

_____

_____

_____

_____

_____

_____

_____

_____

_____

_____

7

2. Identify leading trends that are likely to occur within your industry and develop a plan to be a catalyst for change. Create a system that will allow you to document and reference your new ideas and turn them into the highly prized commercial opportunities.

_____

_____

_____

_____

_____

_____

_____

_____

_____

7

3. Identify what confidence reminders work for you.

7

4. Develop a plan to ensure the CEO and board are aware of your results.

_____

_____

_____

_____

_____

_____

_____

_____

_____

7

5. Identify what leadership skills you can develop to ensure you are perceived as a highly effective leader. This will ensure you are seen as a go to person. This may include: being bolder with your ideas, having greater strategic depth, more influence, effective prioritisation or evolving deliberate planning skills.

7

Conclusion - Being a job magnet

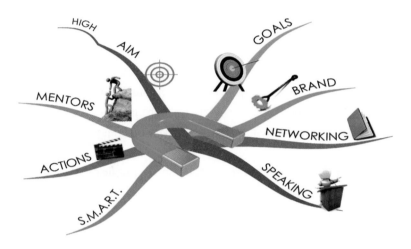

The aim of this book was to equip you with the necessary tools to face the career challenges ahead. In following these 7 simple steps, I believe you will realise your true career potential.

1. Set specific annual career goals that allow you to express your strengths and give you the choice of playing your A game every day. The result being that you will have the autonomy, variety and focus on the work you are passionate about.

2. Set a seemingly 'impossible to achieve' long term career goal, that is ambitious and stretching in its nature. Develop a plan that breaks this goal into manageable steps and adjust your behaviour to move towards its achievement.

3. Develop your personal brand so you can position yourself as a premium employee to attract ideal job opportunities.

4. Develop and utilise a strategic networking plan. This will result in the development of new relationships and job avenues.

5. Have an up to date achievement led CV that is the best possible version of you. Prepare for interviews by researching the interviewer's background and develop a plan to solve their most pressing key business issues.

6. Practice presenting and speaking in public on a regular basis.

7. Use the SMART negotiation formula to ensure you always make the most appropriate career choice and ensure you are appropriately rewarded.

A successful and fulfilling career is the result of deliberate and effective daily thoughts, choices, and actions. Make this year the most transforming and successful in your career!

Develop a specific training plan that incorporates learning from well respected mentors who have achieved the career results you desire. Focus on improving your skills in the areas that are most valued by employers. These include your ability to influence, your results being known to the CEO, being innovative and having an assured confidence in your own ability regardless of economic times.

A final thought – remember that belief in yourself is a very powerful resource to have in your career development toolkit. Aim high, seek new experiences to expand your possibilities and passionately pursue your career goals. Never ever, ever give up.

I wish you the greatest success on your journey.

For further insights and proven methods that give you an unfair advantage in the current job market, visit www.beajobmagnet.co.uk

I will be a job magnet - what I must do in the next 30 days…

References

Bannister, R. (2004) *The Four-Minute Mile.* USA: The Lyons Press viii.

BBC News (2006) *Buffett donates $37billion to charity.*
http://news.bbc.co.uk/1/hi/5115920.stm (11 November 2011).

Buzan, T. And Griffiths, C. (2010). *Mind Maps for Business.*
Harlow: Pearson.

Canfield, J. And Switzer, J. (2005). *The Success Principles.*
New York: HarperCollins.

Carnegie, D. (1936) *How to Win Friends & Influence people.*
New York: Dale Carnegie & Associates, Inc Page 93.

Cialdini, R. (2007) *Influence The Psychology of Persuasion.*
New York: HarperCollins.

Gallo, C. (2010). *The Presentation Secrets of Steve Jobs.*
USA: McGraw-Hill.

Gallo, C. (2011). *The Innovation Secrets of Steve Jobs.*
USA: McGraw-Hill.

Goldstein, N., Martin, S. and Cialdini, R. (2007). *Yes.*
London: Profile Books Limited.

Grout, J. and Perrin, S. (2004) *Mind Games.*
Chichester UK: Capstone Publishing Ltd.

Johnson, S. (2010) *Where Good Ideas Come From.*
http://www.youtube.com/watch?v=NugRZGDbPFU (31 Oct 2011).

Peters, T. (2009) *"Brand You" Thoughts from Tom Peters – Out-Read the Other Guy.*
www.youtube.com/watch?v=rijXiwAQnfl (31 Oct 2011).

Pugh, L. (2010) *Achieving The Impossible.*
London: Simon & Schuster UK Ltd.

Rohn, J. (2011) *Jim Rohn Quotes.*
http://www.brainyquote.com/quotes/authors/j/jim_rohn.html (31 Oct 2011).

Zanartu, R. (2010) Insatiable Musical Curiosity.
Perpetual Spirit 16, 38-44.

Resources

How to craft your ideal career move. Ask yourself the following questions and document your thoughts

What career pathway would you take if you knew you could not fail?

_____

_____

What career aspirations do you secretly dream about?

_____

_____

What career would you love to be doing every day?

_____

_____

What would you like to have achieved by the end of your business career?

_____

_____

Learn from and join the top 10% in your industry

Here's how:

1. Identify the top 10% of people in your industry.

2. Develop a plan of how to connect with those individuals.

3. Connect with them.

Here is an example:

"Hello Jeff, my name is Adrian Evans. We have not met yet. I know you are a busy man, so I will be brief. I own my own Search & Selection business. Over the years you have done an excellent job of building the Robert Half business and moving into the public speaking and coaching arena. I have read and enjoyed a number of your books including 'Mind Games' (2004). I am sure you had many challenges when you were first starting out. I am still at those early stages, trying to figure out everything. Jeff, I would really appreciate if you would spend half hour of your time to answer a few questions."

4. Develop your unique brand pitch and proposition of value added skills and results.

5. Identify the top trends in your industry and prepare plans that solve key decision makers' business problems.

_____

_____

6. Interview and act like the top 10%. Achievers expect to achieve their goals and fully believe they deserve them.

_____

_____

7. Persist until your desired results are achieved.

_____

_____

How to network for career success –
The proven WIN/WIN networking formula

You need to ask yourself the following:

Which 10 people if I networked with would accelerate my career most rapidly?

_____

_____

Identify how you can help this person in their professional or personal life.

_____

_____

Now be flexible.

_____

_____

When connecting with people be completely present.

_____

_____

Integrate social networking into your networking strategy.

_____

_____

Network online with the same integrity and approach as ever offline.

_____

_____

Proven Steps to Your Ideal Role

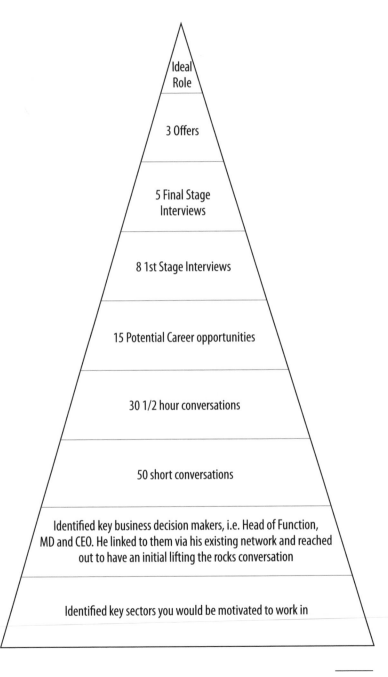

Ideal Role

3 Offers

5 Final Stage Interviews

8 1st Stage Interviews

15 Potential Career opportunities

30 1/2 hour conversations

50 short conversations

Identified key business decision makers, i.e. Head of Function, MD and CEO. He linked to them via his existing network and reached out to have an initial lifting the rocks conversation

Identified key sectors you would be motivated to work in

Successful Interviewing

STAR method - Situation, Task, Action, Result.

Situation: Describe a situation you were involved in that resulted in a positive outcome.

_____

_____

Task: Highlight the tasks that were involved in the situation.

_____

_____

Action: Discuss the variety of actions utilised in the situation's task.

_____

_____

Results: What results directly followed because of your actions?

_____

_____

Quantify your results. Numbers can serve to illustrate your degree of success or level of authority and responsibility very effectively. Also be prepared to provide examples of when results didn't turn out as you planned. What did you do then? What did you learn? Your potential employer will want to see how you react in the face of adversity.

_____

_____

_____

_____

Effective Presentation

Have:

1. A very strong start to provoke curiosity with your audience.

2. Use images and/or music to bring any demonstrations to life.

3. Tell stories that take your audience on an engaging, fun and inspirational journey.

4. Use a 'WOW' moment to leave a lasting positive impression on your future employers.

The SMART system - A proven 5 step framework for making the right decisions in your career and being appropriately rewarded

Start from a well defined plan.

_____

_____

Market yourself as a premium employee.

_____

_____

A range of possible solutions and options.

_____

_____

Re-evaluate all information.

_____

_____

Together have you reached an agreement that works for both parties?

_____

_____

Use the following criteria as a foundation to evaluate the right career move

Criteria	Career Option 1	Career Option 2	Career Option 3
Industry Sector Growth potential			
The Company - its employer brand and reputation			
The challenges & Autonomy of the Role			
Ability of the line manager to realise your potential			
Career Prospects			
Base salary			
Car allowance			
Bonus Potential			

Criteria	Career Option 1	Career Option 2	Career Option 3
How this role fits into your long term career goal and plan			
Location			
Training and personal development potential			
Your Intuition/Gut feeling			
TOTAL			

How to compare different career offers

Criteria	Career Option 1	Career Option 2
Basic Salary		
Bonus		
Other Incentives		
Pension		
Private Medical Insurance		
Life Assurance		
Permanent Health Insurance		
Travel Insurance		
Gym/Club Membership		
Training		
TOTAL		

How to increase your sphere of influence

The 6 weapons are:

1. The Law of reciprocity/reciprocation (give and take)

2. Social proof (does that person comply to the value set of other people?)

3. Authority

4. Commitment and consistency (accepted rules)

5. Liking or being like somebody.

6. Scarcity (the rule of few)

How to be an Innovation leader

Ask yourself the game changing questions such as "What if?" or "Why not?" for great breakthroughs to occur. Incremental steps of change and innovation are achieved with the questions How, What, When and Whom?

_____

_____

Ask yourself could you explore outside your comfort zone for ideas, inspiration and innovation?

_____

_____

How could you create systems to bring these ideas to practical application?

_____

_____

Think about industry blogs, customer forums, look outside your existing sphere of ideas i.e. what are the young generation interested in exploring?

_____

_____

Tools that will help develop your confidence

Expand your existing comfort zone step by step.

_____

_____

Remind yourself of your career successes to date.

_____

_____

Identify feelings of confidence you have previously felt and bring those resources back to your present state of mind.

_____

_____

How to demonstrate key leadership on a daily basis

Walking the walk as well as talking the talk.

_____

_____

Know what gets your people out of bed each day other than just money.

_____

_____

Give people the autonomy to achieve their potential.

_____

_____

Have courage and belief in yourself and others to explore new opportunities.

_____

_____

Be open to and responding effectively to feedback.

_____

_____

7 simple steps to realise your true career potential

1. Set specific annual career goals that allow you to express your strengths and give you the choice of playing your 'A' game every day.

2. Set a seemingly 'impossible to achieve' long term career goal, that is ambitious and stretching in its nature.

3. Develop your personal brand so you can position yourself as a premium employee to attract ideal job opportunities.

4. Develop and utilise a strategic networking plan.

5. Have an up to date achievement led CV that is the best possible version of you. Prepare for interviews by researching the interviewer's background and develop a plan to solve their most pressing key business issues.

6. Practice presenting and speaking in public on a regular basis.

7. Use the SMART negotiation formula to ensure you always make the most appropriate career choice and ensure you are appropriately rewarded.

Develop a training plan that incorporates learning from well respected mentors who have achieved the career results you desire.

For further insights and proven methods that give you an unfair advantage in the current job market, visit www.beajobmagnet.co.uk

Further reading

Bannister, R. (2004) *The Four-Minute Mile*. USA: The Lyons Press.

BBC News (2006) *Buffett donates $37billion to charity*.
http://news.bbc.co.uk/1/hi/5115920.stm (11 November 2011).

Buzan, T. and Griffiths, C. (2010) *Mind Maps for Business*.
Harlow: Pearson.

Canfield, J. and Hansen, M.V. (1994) *Dare To Win*.
New York: Berkley Books.

Canfield, J. and Switzer, J. (2005). *The Success Principles*.
New York: HarperCollins.

Carnegie, D. (1936) *How to Win Friends & Influence people*.
New York: Dale Carnegie & associates Inc.

Cialdini, R. ((2007) *Influence The Psychology of Persuasion*.
New York: HarperCollins.

Dick, F. (2010) *Winning Matters*.
UK: The Abingdon Management Company Limited.

Ellerton, R. (2006) *Live Your Dreams*. UK: Trafford Publishing.

Gallo, C. (2010) *The Presentation Secrets of Steve Jobs*.
USA: McGraw-Hill.

Gallo, C. (2011) *The Innovation Secrets of Steve Jobs*. USA: McGraw-Hill.

Goldstein, N., Martin, S. and Cialdini, R. (2007) *Yes*.
London: Profile Books Limited.

Grout, J. and Perrin, S. (2004) *Mind Games*.
Chichester UK: Capstone Publishing Ltd.

Johnson, S. (2010) *Where Good Ideas Come From*.
http://www.youtube.com/watch?v=NugRZGDbPFU (31 Oct 2011).

Lawless, J. (2008) *Taming tigers*. UK Taming Tigers Publishing.

Orlick, T. (1998) *Embracing Your Potential*. UK: Human Kenetics.

Owen, J. ((2010) *How To Influence*. Harlow UK: Pearson Education Ltd.

Owen, N. (2001) *The Magic of Metaphor*.
Carmarthen Wales: Crown House Publishing.

Peters, T. (2009) *"Brand You" Thoughts from Tom Peters – Out-Read the Other Guy*.
www.youtube.com/watch?v=rijXiwAQnfl (31 Oct 2011).

Pugh, L. (2010) *Achieving The Impossible*.
London: Simon & Schuster UK Ltd.

Rohn, J. (2011) *Jim Rohn Quotes*.
http://www.brainyquote.com/quotes/authors/j/jim_rohn.html
(31 Oct 2011).

Stone, S. (2010) *Love Life Live Life*. London:Piatkus.

Zanartu, R. (2010) Insatiable Musical Curiosity. *Perpetual Spirit (16)*.